MW00423643

Presented To

_____

From

_____

Date

_____

PREPARE YOURSELF TO BE BLESSED

PREPARE YOURSELF TO BE BLESSED

How to PURPOSELY *Enter Into* ABUNDANT LIVING

KEVIN BOYD

DESTINY IMAGE® PUBLISHERS, INC.
P.O. Box 310, Shippensburg, PA 17257-0310

"Promoting Inspired Lives."

This book and all other Destiny Image, Revival Press, MercyPlace, Fresh Bread, Destiny Image Fiction, and Treasure House books are available at Christian bookstores and distributors worldwide.

For a U.S. bookstore nearest you, call 1-800-722-6774.
For more information on foreign distributors, call 717-532-3040.
Reach us on the Internet: www.destinyimage.com.

ISBN 13 TP: 978-0-7684-4105-5
ISBN 13 Ebook: 978-0-7684-8861-6

For Worldwide Distribution, Printed in the U.S.A.

1 2 3 4 5 6 7 / 15 14 13 12

DEDICATION

This book is dedicated to my wife, Gayla, who has been encouraging me for years to put these teachings into book form. She is truly the wind beneath my wings, the love of my life, and the very best that God has to offer.

To my three sons: Austin, Eastin, and Destin, who bring great joy to my heart each day. There is nothing I enjoy more than spending time with you boys. I am so proud to be your dad. Thank you for your honor, love, and support.

ACKNOWLEDGMENTS

My deepest appreciations to...

Mom and Dad, who have always been solid and have taught me the life-changing words of God. Thank you for cheering me on all my life.

All the staff at TCMI. Thank you for doing an amazing job every single week, allowing me to do what I do. You are the best!

All the TCMI family who has dared to dream with me and embraced the vision. "The best is yet to come."

Rosalia Barbosa and Jean Armstrong, who always keep the businesses running smoothly. Thank you for your loyalty and support.

Chanelle Ates, who has spent countless hours on this project pulling everything together and ultimately making me look much smarter than I really am. Your passion for what you do is inspiring, and I am truly grateful.

ENDORSEMENTS

Prepare Yourself to Be Blessed is filled with wisdom and truth. Through this inspiring book, I received new insights into Scriptures I have read hundreds of times. Pastor Boyd has a writing style that is fun and entertaining. He makes you feel like he is sitting next to you telling you a wonderful story. The *God Principles* shared in this book will bless my life for years to come. This inspired book is one I will read again and again.

—Cameron C. Taylor
Founder and President of Multiple Corporations
Bestselling Author of *8 Attributes of Great Achievers*

Pastor Kevin Boyd's new book, *Prepare Yourself to Be Blessed* is like drinking your cup of coffee in the morning with jet-fuel mixed in it. This book gives you the jolt to do the things that you already know you need to do. It propels you off the couch of procrastination and into a lifestyle of decisive action, thus making your highest dreams come to pass. Hope rises with every page you read; it produces a contagious optimism that is reflected in Pastor Kevin's own successful life!

—Reverend Steven Brooks
Author and International Speaker

If you read only one book this year, *Prepare Yourself to Be Blessed* is the one! I could literally feel the clockwork mechanisms falling into place within my life—leading me to want to share my life story and love for Christ! This book needs to be read several times over. Every time I picked it up, new things would open up to me and have new meanings…it is awesome!

—Tom Pappas
Professional Race Car Driver, NHRA Super Comp & TD
CEO Victory Builders & Design Manufacturing
and Installation

Kevin's book immediately captures your attention and is addictive the moment you start reading it. I could not stop, and I read the entire book in one sitting. Suddenly all the missing pieces came together, and I discovered the one or two things I may have missed and that when applied activate super blessing. For anyone who wants to succeed in every area of life, this book is a must-read as it covers areas of success that most success books seem to overlook. If you are serious about being on the cutting edge and joining the ranks of those who have achieved greatness in every sphere of human endeavor, then it could very well be divine providence that has connected you to this book, as you are about to enter a quantum leap in every area of life. Get ready to start moving at warp speed into the highest levels of success and blessing.

—David Herzog
Motivational Speaker
Author of *Natural to SuperNatural Health*

CONTENTS

PREFACE

I believe that every person, regardless of their background, has the ability to live a life that makes a difference and impacts generations to come. As a matter of fact, none of us should leave this planet until we do just that!

From the beginning of time there have always been certain individuals who seem to stand out above the rest. Not all of them were famous—probably most of them unknown to you and me—but if you lived in their little village, town, or city whenever they were alive, you too would have undoubtedly recognized that there was something special about them.

In every culture, in every century, and in every country, from the little islands to the bustling metropolis there have always been people who at first glance might be mislabeled as favored, gifted, or even lucky because of their uncanny ability to always have more than enough. Some may say, "They have the Midas touch," because everything they touch turns to gold.[1]

However, the people closest to them would quickly tell you that it has nothing to do with luck or a fairy tale touch. So then, what is their secret?

Many of them were not born in the palaces of royalty or with a silver spoon in their mouths. Quite the contrary; most of them come from every kind of walk of life. Some have overcome the most horrible circumstances imaginable. Others have conquered stigmas and prejudices. Many simply escaped the routine of mediocrity, but they all stand above the rest and have been recognized by those around them as blessed! Abundantly so!

The same principles that have caused certain individuals to succeed and walk in abundant blessings are available to anyone who will embrace them and consistently walk in them.

However, most people believe that it would take a lucky break or being born under completely different circumstances to make that become a reality for them.

Prepare Yourself to Be Blessed was written to shatter misconceptions and take anyone who is willing to go on a journey that will surely lead them into the fulfillment of their God-given potential. The keys and divine principles released in this book will work for an electrician, as well as the entrepreneur. It will work for the factory worker the same as it works for the lawyer.

No matter where you're starting from, these principles will undoubtedly take you to places that you might have once thought unobtainable.

Clear your mind, open up your heart, and prepare yourself to be blessed!

Endnote

1. Midas Touch, originated 1880-1885; http://www.usingenglish.com/reference/idioms/midas+touch.html.

INTRODUCTION

It's a peculiar thing to think about—how to prepare yourself to be blessed. When I mention it to people, most of them look at me as if I've just spoken to them in an unfamiliar language. For many years, I have taught on the subject of preparing yourself to be blessed and have seen lives miraculously changed by the consistent following of certain principles.

This book is my attempt to reach as many people as possible with some life-changing fundamentals, which will indeed transform mentalities and impact futures!

Everybody wants to be blessed, but very few have considered this truth: it takes real preparation to truly be able to handle and enjoy blessings.

Blessed is not lucky. Blessed is not coincidence. Blessed is directly relative to your cooperation with *God Principles* (whether you believe in God or not). We are all blessed to a certain extent, but the people we consider extremely blessed are not where they are by accident.

As a matter of fact, I truly believe that most people are living at a level of blessings that is equal to their preparation. Now with that said, it is important that we don't automatically transpose the words blessing or blessed to mean money. Blessings definitely do include finances, but are much more expansive than finances alone.

It takes real preparation to truly be able to handle and enjoy blessings.

Blessings are ultimately from the Lord, and according to various Scriptures combined, you frequently hear the phrase, "God will never put more on you than you can bear." Now I know using that particular saying in this context might have caused you to raise an eyebrow, but it's very true.

As a matter of fact, many times we look at the Scriptures in the more negative viewpoint when, in actuality, this interpretation would tend to be more accurate than the common understanding. The common understanding of this is that God will not allow more hardship to come upon us than we are able to endure. However, that is only true in the sense that we are able to ultimately handle it because of His strength and not our own. Consider this alternate viewpoint for a moment and think about God not giving us more than we can handle when it comes to blessings, prosperity, relationships, positions, and so forth. There are specifically designed *God Principles* that have been made available to every person—regardless of background, ethnicity, and gender—that must be learned and practiced if you truly want to enjoy the blessing of the Lord to the fullest.

Or what man is there among you who, if his son asks for bread, will give him a stone? Or if he asks for a fish, will he give him a serpent? If you then, being evil, know how to give good gifts to your children, how much more will your Father who is in heaven give good things to those who ask Him! (Matthew 7:9-11)

I have read these verses time and time again, but it wasn't until a few years ago that I truly began to dissect what they were really saying. At the same time, I was also acknowledging before God that we do not always get what we ask for. I couldn't help but wonder, *Why not?* It was in this time of prayer and meditation that God revealed to me a new revelation and understanding of this passage, which I found to be absolutely fascinating.

This new revelation helped me to realize that many times God will not give us many of the things we desire and ask for simply because *we are not prepared to receive or handle them!* It's not that God doesn't desire to bless us. For He declares in

His Word (the Bible), *"It is your Father's good pleasure to give you the kingdom"* (Luke 12:32). Over and over again, Scriptures throughout the Bible repeat that God not only desires to bless us, but actually delights in or takes pleasure in blessing His children (see Num. 14:8, 2 Sam. 22:20, 1 Kings 10:9, Ps. 16:11, Ps. 18:19, Ps. 35:27).

So then, why don't we always see the blessings? Why do we not receive many of the things we ask for? The issue is not with God; the issue is with us! Many times God will not release to us the things that we ask for simply because we are not prepared to receive them. He recognizes that, even though we think we're prepared and we think that what we are asking for is bread, many times it is actually a snake, or it can become a snake shortly after we receive it.

"I want to bless you, but as a loving Father, I will not give you a snake!"

Let me put it like this: in our limited understanding (meaning that many times we are only seeing a small sliver of the whole picture), we think we can handle it. We think we're ready for it, because we are comparing our request to our limited understanding of the picture. However, God in His infinite wisdom and understanding, who sees the whole picture perfectly and clearly, can see the things that we cannot yet even comprehend. And in His great compassion and love for us He says:

I want to bless you. I want to prosper you. I want to increase you, but this would not ultimately do any of that. You're not ready for it, you haven't fully prepared yourself to receive this amount of financial increase, this kind of life-long relationship, this position of responsibility or leadership, so I cannot as a loving Father, release it to you. I will not give you a snake!

Think about what I'm saying for a minute. How many times have you seen people receive something, which sounded like it should have been great, should have helped them grow, should have helped them move forward, but instead it became a big mess?

My case in point—lottery winners. How many times have we seen or heard about a family that wins a ton of money and five years later they end up worse off than before? Not only do they usually end up in worse financial shape (having now incurred all kinds of debt), but many times the family itself ends up in shambles because they have fought over the money, started to not trust each other, and pushed people away. That snake bit everyone involved, leaving them all dying from the poison of unpreparedness![1]

Another example is our multimillionaire superstars. How many times do we see someone's talent take them farther than their overall character? Before long, we end up seeing a very rich walking disaster.[2] People who reach tremendous levels of financial status or high levels of position and power without being prepared for it become the most miserable people in the world. They must quickly begin to correct these issues by following *God Principles*, or they will be destroyed by the snake's bite.

It's true that many people follow and practice these principles without even knowing the principles' true origin. Regardless, they work. On the other hand, it must be very frustrating to have loads of money and earthly possessions galore, yet be sad, lonely, fearful, and addicted. What a tragedy—having everything that we've been told would make everything A-OK, yet we find ourselves in the midst of another divorce, getting arrested again, going to jail for another DUI or for abusing our significant other. Rich people are not guaranteed happiness, but blessed people are always full of joy![3]

How about with our children? We can easily see how this perspective is important in their development. As a matter of fact, as adults, many times we need to go back to some of the things that we were told were important as children. Like reading, playing nice together, and most importantly, having someone tell us (even if that someone is ourselves), "No, you aren't ready for that." Reaching the age of 21, 30, 45, or even 50 does not automatically qualify us for anything really. We can easily look at our children and say, "You're just not ready for this. Maybe when you're a little older and more mature we'll talk about that." Yet when we turn 18 and move out, we are supposedly ready for anything and everything.[4] Somehow I don't think it works that way! You see, we should always see ourselves as children when it comes to our relationship with God. We never reach an age (or at least we shouldn't) when we move out of God's house and are all grown up and on our own!

The problem is that we have this unwritten law in our society that says when we reach 18 or 21 that we're pretty much qualified for anything. However, in the world of divine laws and principles, there is no such age. In other words, there is not necessarily any automatics with our heavenly Father. This ultimately means that, with God, one person may receive at 20 years old what another person won't receive until age 52. Why? It's simple, really. The blessings are released to those who have prepared themselves to receive them by embracing and cooperating with *God Principles!* On the other hand, to not embrace these principles while at the same time increasing in possessions, wealth, or position can be absolutely disastrous.

We would never, as responsible parents, let a toddler play with a loaded gun. We would also probably agree that it is very unwise to give a 14-year-old son the keys to a sports car and say, "Hey, load it up with a bunch of your friends tonight and take it out for a spin."

But many times, that's exactly what we're asking God to give or to do for us. We ask for things that we are simply not prepared to handle. There does, however, come a time in people's lives when they could receive a gun for a birthday gift without anyone being concerned for their lives. There is also a time that a young man can handle a sports car responsibly, but with training, experience, and maturity serving as prerequisites for such gifts.

Many times, even though we are sincere in our asking, sincere in our belief that we are ready, God simply will not release to us our request because He sees the things that we cannot see. He sees in full, while we see in part.

Over and over, we witness on the news those who have received much bread before being prepared. We have seen things that made us shake our heads in disbelief, causing us to say, "How could they throw it all away for something so stupid? How could they let themselves get caught up in something like that when they have so much going for them? Why would they risk everything for so little? They are so talented! So successful! I just don't get it," And before long we see that the bread was not bread for them at all; instead we see the effects of a poisonous bite, another needless tragedy, a life in shambles.

Many of us (maybe in a smaller way) could easily end up with similar results, if God were to release to us now the things that we have been eagerly asking for.

This might be hard to understand at the moment, but sometimes a "no" from God can be a *huge* blessing! There's an old country western song that says, "Some of God's greatest gifts are unanswered prayers." Garth Brooks nailed it on that one. It is very, very true.

Remember, it pleases God to bless you. So get ready to embrace and practice the *God Principles* in this book and prepare yourself to be blessed!

Endnotes

1. "Links to Various Sad But True Winners Stories," *The Lotto Report*; http://www.lottoreport.com/sadbuttrue.htm; accessed August 22, 2011.

2. "Highly Paid Stars in Trouble," *The Roar*; http://www.theroar.com.au/2009/03/14/high-paid-stars-in-trouble/; accessed August 22, 2011.

3. "Too Rich for Your Health?" WebMD Feature; http://www.medicinenet.com/script/main/art.asp?articlekey=50794; accessed August 22, 2011.

4. Society's Definition of adulthood: http://www.uic.edu/depts/comm/lifehist/LHMPUnderSociology.html.

Chapter 1

WHAT DO YOU CALL IT?

It seems appropriate that we would find our first *God Principle* in Genesis. In fact, Genesis not only records *the beginning*, but it also records God's intentions for humankind and the intimate supernatural relationship we were designed to walk in. From the very beginning we see God creating a paradise and placing people within this magnificent place.

Immediately, we see that God desires people to be blessed, to live without lack, and to enjoy life all around. Yet at the same time, this garden paradise was not designed for people to lay around all day in hammocks drinking lemonade (we'll get into more of this in the last part of the book). Some of God's initial dialog with people after blessing them and telling them to be fruitful and multiply, was instructions on *tending and keeping* the Garden.

Get this: God had just finished creating absolutely everything, clearly showing that He didn't need any help from anyone to do anything. Yet, He turns right around and lets Adam know that it's vital that he participate in this whole process. It's what I like to call the *Power of Cooperation*. Our part is very small compared to His, yet the power of us cooperating with Him is infinite!

I like to say it like this, "If you'll do what you can do, God will do what you cannot!"

It is so very important that we establish this understanding before we begin to unlock these principles that will inevitably change our lives. Why? Because all *God Principles* take more than revelation; they also require participation. They are first realized, but then activated by us doing our part. I like to call this one, the *Name It Principle*:

> *Then the Lord God said, "It is not good for the man to be alone; I will make a helper who is right for him." The Lord God formed all the wild animals and all the birds out of the ground. Then He brought them to the man to see what he would call them. Whatever the man called each creature, became its name. So the man named all the domestic animals, all the birds, and all the wild animals. But the man found no helper who was right for him. So the Lord God caused him to fall into a deep sleep. While the man was sleeping, the Lord God took one of the man's ribs and closed up the flesh at that place. Then the Lord God formed a woman from the rib that He had taken from man. He brought her to the man* (Genesis 2:18-22 GW).

Did you happen to pick up on anything as you read those five verses? Did God's order of creation seem a bit odd after revealing His thoughts? Read them again and you'll see what I mean.

**If you'll do what you can do,
God will do what you cannot!**

Even if you are not particularly familiar with the Bible, it's fairly easy to see what I'm talking about here. God decides that *it is not good for man to be alone*, so He comes up with a plan. He decides to create a companion for Adam. Not just a *helper*, but the very thing He knew Adam needed most: a special someone to connect with. Someone designed to fulfill him and give him the ability to multiply, to be stronger, and to do even greater things than if he were alone.

But then God does a peculiar thing. Right there in the middle of announcing His big plan to Adam, God switches gears. The next thing we know, He's making animals—*domestic animals, wild animals, and birds*—out of the very dirt He had just created a few days before!

Now why in the world would He do that? Wouldn't it make more sense if He went straight to the part where He forms a woman out of Adam's rib? But He doesn't! And for the first time, I started to wonder, *Why?* And as I began to think and to pray about this question, God began to show me something I have never seen before.

God revealed His plan to create the person we later come to know in the story as Eve. Now let me tell you a little something about Eve. She is not just a companion; she's not just Adam's new friend. Eve represents the very best that God has to offer. She's the one thing that God knows that Adam needs the most.

Eve represents *the very best* God has to offer.

What about for you? What does God desire to give to you? There is something that God has for you that, like Eve, represents the best possible choice, gift, or solution for your life— something that God knows will help you become everything He created you to be. Now, I'll tell you, I don't know anyone who doesn't hope and pray to find the very best that life has to offer them. So, can you imagine what went through Adam's mind as he listened to God's plan?

The suspense must have been through the roof and his excitement off the chart. Adam is about to burst with expectation, but before God delivers this precious gift—He stops and seems to head off in a completely different direction. He suddenly switches gears and starts creating animals. And then He does something really odd, He starts bringing the animals to Adam to see what he would name them.

Now I don't know about you, but I find it interesting that the God of the universe, the Creator of everything, the One with infinite wisdom, absolute knowledge, and unlimited understanding would take the time to bring His masterpiece sculptures to Adam. And yet that is exactly what He did. Why is that? Our answer is found here:

> *The Lord God had formed all the wild animals and all the birds out of the ground. Then He brought them to the man to see what he would call them. Whatever the man called each creature, became its name. So the man named all the domestic animals, all the birds, and all the wild animals. But the man found no helper who was right for him* (Genesis 2:19-20 GW).

There's a concept here that shows that God has put one of His principles in place that very much determines reality as we know it. Again, I call it the *Name It Principle*. It is the principle of creation. God used this principle when He created everything. Then, He gave it to us. Now, I'm going to go between the lines and get a little extra-biblical here. Until recently, I've had an image in my mind of how the activities of these verses must have unfolded.

Let me paint the picture as I've always seen it, and let's see if this is kind of how you've always imagined it as well.

Imagine God leading this massive beast to Adam: gigantic paws, a wild mane, a deep, menacing roar. The creature exudes raw power.

"Come here, Adam," God calls, "I have something to show you. Take a look at this."

Wow! Adam thinks as he takes a quick step back, *That's one big animal!*

"I want you to name it for Me, Adam," He says, "Go ahead—give it a shot. What do you call it?" Adam thinks a minute, glad that God is holding the beast in check.

"Lion!" he declares.

"Great name!" God smiles as He ruffles the creature's mane and sends Mr. Lion ambling off into the brush.

How am I doing? Is this anything close to how you imagined this Genesis scene unfolding? However, as I sat reading those verses, really thinking about what they said, a new picture began to form in my mind:

God reaches down and grabs a handful of dirt. His fingers move over the mass as He squeezes and shapes it into a form. After a while of perfecting each detail, He looks up.

"Adam." He says. "Come here a minute. I have something to show you." As He steps back from what He's been working on, Adam gets his first peek, as God reveals a perfectly sculpted, beautifully detailed piece of clay (dirt).

As Adam intensely scans this magnificent sculpture, he curiously asks, "What is it, Lord?"

"You tell Me," God smiles.

"What?" Adam's not sure he understands.

"Name it, son." So Adam takes a long look at the master-piece that God has just created. He takes in the long neck, the tiny ears, and the yellow-orange spots.

"What do you call it?" He urges.

Adam takes another thoughtful look. "I call you…Giraffe," he speaks to the lump of dirt standing lifeless before God.

"Giraffe," God muses. "It's catchy; I like it. Giraffe it is!"

And with that, God breathes into the sculpture, and His magnificent creation springs to life.

God reaches down again and scoops up another handful of clay. He presses; He molds. Finally He's finished.

"What do you call this one, Adam?" He asks. Adam rubs his chin as he takes in the large, bulky body, the long snout, the big floppy ears, the tiny little tail.

Hmm… he thinks, "Elephant! I call you, Elephant." And as he spoke it, so it was. God breathes on the inert mass of dirt, and it too springs to life.

Adam clears his throat. "Umm…God?" he asks as he watches Elephant lumber off into the bushes, "is that my helpmate?"

"No, no, no, no, no," God answers with a smile. "Don't get ahead of Me now, Adam. Focus, boy, focus! We have work to do."

**Adam must have thought
he died and went to Heaven
when he got a look at Eve!**

On and on it goes. One by one God fashions each animal out of dirt. And when they were just right, He brings them to Adam. Each, a masterpiece, was just waiting to be named so it can come to life. But don't you know that with every new creature, Adam wondered, *Is this the one? Is this my helpmate? Is this my special companion?*

You see, Adam had no idea what his special gift, his best, would look like. He didn't have the convenience of knowing the end of the story as we do. All he knew was that the last thing God had said was that He was going to make him a helper that would complete him. And because no one else existed, he had no idea what this helper was going to be like. All he knew is that at some point, one of those special creations would be his promise come to life. I must inject here, however, that after seeing Hippos, Donkeys, and Hyenas, Adam must have thought he died and went to Heaven when he got a look at Eve!

**The Creator was teaching
the created how to create.**

The Bible doesn't say how long all of this molding and breathing and naming took, but it must have been a very long and tedious task. I know I wouldn't want that job! Think about it: What must it have been like? Did Adam put thought into each one, or after a while, did he just pick something, *anything*, just to get it over with? Maybe the animals with real long, interesting names—like Hippopotamus, Rhinoceros, and Elephant—were named first while Adam was still inspired. And after months, maybe years of naming, we ended up with Dog, Cat, Rat...*next!* I guess that's just one of those questions we won't have answers for until we get over on the other side. I do know this for sure; whatever Adam called them is exactly what they became.

As I thought about this scenario—this possibility—I realized something. Tucked in between *the promise* and *the fulfillment*, was a principle and a process that still holds true today.

The Creator was teaching the created how to create and how to establish something through the spoken word. Now, Adam didn't learn how to physically create an animal, but with each new name, God was showing Adam how to establish a reality out of something that, until then, had only been a possibility.

You see, an eagle was just another lump of earth until Adam said, "I call you Eagle." A dog and an elephant were simply two different shapes of dirt until Adam put a name to them. But once he did that and God breathed on them, they were created. Once he had spoken a name, that is what they became. And because of that name, they became real.

If you doubt that, imagine this: you and a friend are outside watching a woman walk her little dog. Pointing at the dog, you turn to your friend and say, "Hey, look at that interestingly shaped piece of dirt!" Now if the woman hears you, you're in trouble! Why? Because her dog isn't a piece of dirt.

He's a dog! He has a reality. And once something has been spoken into being, it has a reality. You can't go around calling things that are as if they are not. Neither can you go around calling things that are not as if they are. Or can you?

Now you very well may be thinking: *What in the world are you talking about? I mean, it's really nice that Adam called the animals by names, but how does this help me? What does this*

*have to do with what I'm going through? 'Cause I'll tell you, the
bills are stacking up and I'm dealing with real fear, real anxiety,
and real depression. I need something that will help me overcome,
something that will help me break through, something to help me
turn things around. Come on now; I like dogs as much as the next
person, but what are you talking about here?*

I'm really glad you asked! This creation principle of *Naming
It,* is not just something that God cooked up for Adam and the
animals. It's real. And whether you recognize it or not, whether
you understand it or not, whether you even know it or not, this
is one of those *God Principles* that is alive and well and working
in your life right now. And because it is a God Principle, it is
as real and as powerful today as it was when God first taught
it to Adam. You see, just like He did with Adam, God is still
bringing things to all of His people, every single day, to ask,
"What do you call it?" Every 24 hours the sun peaks up over
the horizon. In essence, God walks up to you and shows you a
brand-new day. He asks, "What do you call it?" And my friend,
whatever you call it is exactly what it will become.

I see it happen every day. God brings an opportunity to one
person. "What do you call it?" He asks.

"Too difficult!" says the person. "Can't be done!"

He brings the same opportunity to a different person who
takes one look at it and yells, "Are you kidding me? I've been
looking for this for years! Let me at it!"

We've all seen it: same opportunity, different names. What one person calls *junk*, another calls *treasure*. What one person calls *obligation* another calls *privilege*.

A friend is running a little late for the lunch appointment he set up a few days earlier. When he finally arrives, looking somewhat embarrassed, one person might say, *"It's about time!"* Another person says, *"I'm so glad we have this opportunity to get together!"*

One person has a long day at work and on the way home says, "It's too much work, this job stinks." While his co-worker (who experienced the same difficulties that day) now reflects on her way home and quietly whispers, *"Thank You, God, for my job!"* The same 24 hours called by two different names are as different as day and night. Let me show you how:

One guy, we'll call him George, wakes up in the morning.

"Ahh!" he screeches. "Stupid alarm clock didn't go off again!"

He jumps out of bed and stubs his toe on the dresser. Man, is he late! He brushes his teeth in the shower, throws on clothes, and grabs his briefcase. There's no time to eat. He drops his keys and they slide under the couch, as he bends down to find them, he realizes his socks don't match. There's no time to change them; they will have to do. "Man!" he fumes. "I can tell already. This is going to be a *horrible day!*"

The very same day across town, Fred wakes up to a phone call from his precious wife whom he loves and adores.

"Honey," she tells him, "I know it's your day off, and I wanted you to sleep in. I'm just calling to let you know I made you a pot of coffee…and guess what? I bought your favorite muffins. They're right next to the coffee pot. Now don't sleep too late; I scheduled a massage for you at noon. I want you to have the best day ever. And, oh, by the way, the Income Tax check came, and we got back an extra $5,000! Isn't God good? Have a great day!"

Fred rolls over with a happy sigh. "I can already tell," he announces, "this is going to be a *really great day!*"

But I want to let you in on a little revelation I had. God doesn't create good days or bad days or even in-between days. He just creates days, indifferent days that take on the character and the flavor of whatever you choose to name them.

Don't allow the circumstances around you to dictate what you name the indifferent day that God created for you. You have the opportunity and the ability to create good days, good things, a good marriage, good relationships, a good life, at any moment of your day, all because there is a God Principle in place that says you can.

Don't allow the circumstances around you to dictate what you name the indifferent day that God created for you. Don't let a stubbed toe or a muffin on the counter give your day a name. Forget about the circumstances. Say as King David did in the Psalms, *"This is the day that the Lord has made. I will rejoice and be glad in it"* (Ps. 118:24).

I wonder what would happen if all this next week, starting tomorrow morning, you decided to greet each morning with an outrageous expression of joy. Maybe it could start something like this:

(snoring…snoring…beep…beep… alarm) Yeeeee hahahaha! This is going to be the best day ever! This is the day that the Lord has made! I will rejoice! Wooo hooo! I will be glad!

I promise you, if you start your day like that, something will change! Mark my words.

Right, Kevin! I can hear you thinking from here. *I'm really going to leap out of bed and run around the house like a crazy person first thing in the morning. Give me a break!*

OK, OK. I know I'm being extreme here, but ask yourself why you are so willing to accept the alternative. Maybe it's time to try something different. If nothing else, wake up and laugh for two minutes. Just start going *Ha! Ha! Hahaha!* Get it going—let it build up some steam. Just do something!

God creates a day, but we create good days. Take the time to decide and declare that *this day is going to be amazing.* Just make sure you warn your spouse you are going to do it! Then do something to start each day consciously harnessing the power of your own thoughts and words. It will make a world of a difference in your life.

Now, this does not immunize you from challenges. God knows that there are going to be challenges in your life. He knows what it's like to be here on earth. He understands troubles and trials and fires and temptations. And because He knows what it's like to be human, He gave us a special gift to help us get through. It's called *faith*.

**Call those things that
are not as if they are.**

The Bible teaches that every person has been given a measure of faith. You have a measure of faith in you. Why? Because God knew that if you would just activate your faith, even on your bad days, even when circumstances are threatening to mess up your day that your faith would allow you to see past the troubles, trials, and temptations and help you *call those things that are not as if they are.*

Let me give you an example: Let's say you lose your job. What's the first thing you do? The smart thing to do is activate that measure of faith in you and use it to call up a new, better job. Tomorrow morning when you wake up, you put your feet on the floor, jump up, and say out loud, "Thank you, God, for a brand-new job!"

Okay, let me get this straight…You want me to thank God for a new job that I don't have yet?

Yes, that's exactly what I want you to do—and I'll tell you why. You see, there is something very important that you need to understand. Your words have power. In fact, they are so powerful that when you speak, your words put Heaven in motion. Why? Because it's a God Principle. There wasn't a *hippopotamus* until Adam said, "Hippopotamus!" When you wake up in the morning, you have two choices: you can call your day, your job, your life, *lost*—or you can call it *blessed*.

Think about this: You get up in the morning. You lost your job the day before. You sit up and you say, "Thank You, God, for a great new job…*I call it in, today!*" You've barely gotten the words out of your mouth and—*KABOOM!* Heaven stands at attention. The angels look at God, and He says, "You heard it! He activated the *Name It Principle*. Go make it happen."

As fanciful as it may sound, this really is pretty much how it happens. But let me qualify it: some people think that all they have to do is *Name It* and claim it, blab it and grab it.

They think, *Great! I'm going to name it, and before I finish this chapter, I'll have my whatever-it-is-I'm-believing-for…* But there's a catch. You see, I don't know how long it took Adam to name the animals, but I know it had to have taken awhile. Day after day, species after species, Adam looked and named and looked again and thought up another name. Lion, Horse, Alligator, Canary, Bass... *Is she here yet?* Wallaby, Camel, Gnat... on and on and on. Even when he felt like quitting, he didn't; he just kept going. When it came to applying the *Name It Principle,* Adam was faithful and consistent, and because of that, Adam received God's best for his life.

OK, I see it! I can taste it! I'm excited! I'm ready! Let me at it!

Well, good. But before you run off and get started naming things, I should probably mention this one particular point. It is both the good news and the not-so-good news. You see, regardless of the content, this principle works. It works for you to help you move forward in your life, and it works in reverse, against you. The same principle that is activated by your positive words is also activated by your negative words.

You've lost your job. You wake up in the next morning, your feet hit the floor, and you declare, "Thank You, God, for a great new job." You get up, you brush your teeth, drink your coffee, check the newspaper, and start sending out resumes.

Three days later, no job yet, and you're starting to get a little frustrated. Ten days later, you're still sending out resumes, but now you're grumbling, "I hate this! This is stupid! I've sent out a hundred resumes and nothing happened! I can't even find a stupid job! This God Principle stuff doesn't work! All for some stupid, stupid job!"

The first few times you say *stupid* the angels look at God. He rolls His eyes. "Just…wait," He tells them. "We're going to give him that one. He's a good kid. He'll snap out of it."

Another day goes by, and you're still stuck on *stupid*. The angels look at God. "This," He tells them, "is why I made grace. But don't worry. It will be OK."

Two weeks later and your name has stuck. "OK," God tells the angels. "You heard him. He wants a stupid job—go ahead and give it to him!"

Some situations take more time than others to shift and change. That's why it is so important to be faithful and consistent when using God's principles. You faithfully believe for a great job.

You go to job fairs, you go on interviews, put out resumes. You name your job great and your life blessed. Days go by and things start to change. You don't see it yet, but it's there, just under the surface. People and positions start shifting around.

A manager wants to move back to Connecticut to be near her aging parents; the person next up for the promotion receives a windfall and quits. The next in line becomes a missionary and moves to Brazil. Everything is lining up for you to have your super, great, incredible, amazing job when suddenly, you get tired of waiting.

"I've had it!" you yell, "This is stupid! Stupid, stupid, stupid!" And eeerk! Everything comes to a screeching halt. All the good you've been building up starts breaking down. Oh, you'll still get the job—but now it's not the great one; it's the stupid one, because you've put in your new order. The *Name It Principle* is still working, but this time, it's working against you—just like you told it to!

This principle isn't just for finding a job. It works for everything else as well. "Stupid alarm never goes off!" It's probably going to keep on doing just that. "My boss is so mean!" Keep saying that—it's sure to make him much friendlier. "My brother-in-law is such a jerk!" The more you say that, the more jerkiness comes out of him.

Don't complicate your life and destroy your destiny by causing God's principles to work against you. Even if that new job has not come in the first week, don't start putting adjectives in front of it when you talk about it: "Stupid job! There's nothing good out there…" That kind of talk does nothing but break down and destroy what you were building. You literally create unnecessary havoc in your life by allowing the wrong words to come out of your mouth. You keep saying, "My marriage is on the rocks. My marriage is rocky. My marriage is on its last leg." That is exactly what you will get.

You keep telling that kid of yours who keeps getting in trouble, "You're going to end up in jail, boy. They're going to lock you away." And guess where he's going to end up?

We keep saying these things. "I feel a lump. It's probably cancer… This lump is probably cancer." And guess what? That lump is probably cancer because your words are powerful. When spoken, they are designed to create things that do not yet exist.

Do you remember that little kid song? "Oh be careful little mouth what you say. Oh, be careful little mouth what you say. There's a Father up above looking down in tender love, Oh be careful…" You thought it was just talking about cuss words! Now granted, cuss words have no place in your life, but in my opinion, calling a day *bad* is worse than cussing. You're talking about your destiny; you're talking about your life! Calling your marriage hopeless is unbelievably bad. Calling your job lame is a setup for a problem. Calling your opportunities too difficult, calling your volunteer work at church small and insignificant—this is deadly stuff. The power of life and death is in your tongue (see Prov. 18:21).

Choose life that you may live!

God forms the possibility of something, but it's up to you to form and create the reality of it and then draw it into your life. That is one of the reasons why it is so important to speak words that are even greater than your own. If you're going to create something, wouldn't it be smart to use the best building materials available?

When you speak the words of God, angels go into action.

When you plant God's words in your heart and you begin to use God's own words to create your life, you've taken it to a whole other level. That's because when you speak the words of God, angels go into action. When you speak the words of God, life goes into motion. When you speak the words of God, all kinds of good things get released into your life—things like healing, faith, hope, love, and patience.

Let me show you what I mean. Read the next few verses out loud. All of them come from the Book of Psalms. Don't just mumble through then—declare them. Remember, words have the power to create, so put some feeling into it!

This is the day that the Lord has made. I will rejoice and be glad in it (Psalm 118:24).

The Lord is my strength and my song, and He has become my salvation (Psalm 118:14).

The LORD is my light and my salvation; whom shall I fear? The LORD is the strength of my life; of whom shall I be afraid? (Psalm 27:1)

God is our refuge and stregth, a very present help in trouble (Psalm 46:1).

But You, O Lord, are a shield for me. my glory and the One who lifts up my head (Psalm 3:3).

He leads me beside still waters. He restores my soul. I will not lack any good thing (Psalm 23: 2-3, 34:10).

He is my provider, my peace and my healer. With God I have victory. Nothing is impossible with God (Genesis

24:14; Psalm 29:11; Exodus 15:26; Psalm 30:2 107:20, 147:3; Isaiah 53:5; 1 Choronicles 59:11; 1 Corinthians 15:55-57; 1 John 5:4).

Can you feel the atmosphere starting to change? You see, when you use God's own words to create, things change. Try it again.

Now you can't tell me that you didn't feel that! This is my secret weapon for overcoming discouragement or fear. In fact, anytime I feel negative about myself or my situation, I start speaking God's words. I say out loud:

My heart is not troubled. I am liberated from all negative influences. No chain can hold me. No yoke can bind me, because I am more than a conqueror. I am unshakable. I am unmovable. I am unstoppable. I am daily loaded with blessings (see John 14:27 KJV; Gal. 5:1 AMP; Ps. 107:14; Acts 16:26; Isa. 9:4; Gal. 5:1; Rom. 8:37; John 16:31 MSG; Ps. 16:8, 18:29, 68:19).

And my personal favorite: I can do all things through Christ who is my strength (see Phil. 4:13).

You don't have to be in church to do this. You can start right where you are. Consciously choose to speak words that bless and bring life to you and into your life. I can't even begin to tell you the difference it will make in your life.

King David (the writer of many of the Psalms) understood this principle. He knew that the spoken word was powerful.

That's one of the reasons why God called David *"a man after My own heart"* (Acts 13:22). David also understood that it went much deeper than simple head knowledge; it went deeper than positive thinking. David knew that the real secret to making the power of words work in his life was this: it had to get into his heart. That's why he wrote, *"I have hidden Your word in my heart, O God"* (Ps. 119:11).

Years later when Jesus walked the earth, He taught the same thing when He said that it was out of the abundance of the heart that the mouth speaks (see Luke 6:45). Let me put it into today's language:

> *Whatever is in your heart will be revealed and declared through your mouth. And that which you speak, will be what you create.*

You will create with what is in your heart. If that's a problem for you, change what's in your heart.

Is it all coming together for you? I hope so! You will create with what is in your heart. If that's a problem for you, change what's in your heart. Invest some time and effort into filling yourself up with good things. Many people spend so much time investing in other things, how about investing in your inner person, your spirituality—the rewards are literally out of this world!

Now, this is not a guarantee that you will never have problems. In fact, I can promise you that you will! But when you understand the power of your words and you take responsibility for your situation, you can activate the *Name It Principle* to change and adjust your atmosphere and your situation.

All hell can be breaking loose; you can have your back up against a corner and see no way out; your friends can say what Job's wife said, "just curse God and die" (see Job 2:9). But if you will choose your words carefully and exercise your God-given measure of faith and begin to call into reality the possibilities of each day, it will all work out for your good.

Don't wait for circumstances to change before you begin declaring good things over your life. Declare today that your health is getting better. Declare today that your marriage is getting stronger. Declare it today that your financial life is improving. Declare today that your best days are still ahead.

Declare today that this is the day that the Lord has made. I will rejoice. I will call it a good day!

Chapter 2

What Do You Have in Your House?

A certain woman of the wives of the sons of the prophets cried out to Elisha, saying, "Your servant my husband is dead, and you know that your servant feared the Lord. And the creditor is coming to take my two sons to be his slaves." So Elisha said to her, "What shall I do for you? Tell me, what do you have in the house?" And she said, "Your maidservant has nothing in the house but a jar of oil." Then he said, "Go, borrow vessels from everywhere, from all your neighbors—empty vessels; do not gather just a few. And when you have come in, you shall shut the door behind you and your sons; then pour it into all those vessels, and set aside the full ones." So she went from him and shut the door behind her and her sons, who brought the vessels to her; and she poured it out. Now it came to pass, when the vessels were full, that she said to her son, "Bring me another vessel." And he said to her, "There is not another vessel." So the oil ceased. Then she came and told the man of God. And he said, "Go, sell the oil and pay your debt; and you and your sons live on the rest" (2 Kings 4:1-7).

I have spoken on this passage many times over the years, but I have never unlocked what I am about to share with you until now. Take a second look at that first verse:

A certain woman of the wives of the sons of the prophets cried out to Elisha, saying, "Your servant my husband is dead, and you know that your servant feared the Lord. And the creditor is coming to take my two sons to be his slaves."

Think about that for a moment, doesn't this strike you as odd? Focus on this widow's deceased husband for a moment; here is a righteous man, a devout servant of the Lord in service to the prophet Elisha. He is a man of position—a prophet or, at the very least, a prophet-in-training. He passes away and because of his great debt, his two sons are about to be thrust into a life of slavery. You see, in his day, slavery was literal. His family was about to be shattered and torn apart. Now, this was thousands of years ago, but oddly enough, this same scene plays out each and every day in our modern society. Today it's metaphorical, of course, but families are still being torn apart and shattered by debt, and it has to stop!

Don't spend your life looking for the miracle without recognizing what got you into the place of needing one.

I want to say this clearly: It *was* not and *is* not God's will or plan for any of His people to be enslaved by debt. It is not His plan for you to live or to die in so much debt that it threatens to destroy or greatly alter the ability of those you leave behind to function or to progress once you are gone. But barring a miracle that is exactly what was about to happen to this widow woman and her family.

Now you have the ability to look through this whole story here, to see the miracle and the end results, and to think that everything works out great. The thing that most people miss is this: if you become like the widow and spend your life looking for the miracle, you will never recognize what got you into the place of needing one.

In pleading her case to Elisha the prophet, the widow tells us why she needed one. She begins to reveal a flawed mentality. In doing that, she shows us the root of the problem, and here it is: "Elisha," she says, "*your* servant, my husband, is dead. Elisha, you know that *your* servant feared the Lord." Are *you* picking it up yet?

"My husband was *your* servant. *You know* that he was a good man. *You know* that he feared God. *You know, you know, you know*…and now the creditors are coming to take my sons away."

Elisha replies, "What shall I do for you?" Or to put it another way, *"Why is this my problem?"*

Elisha's simple question back to her, *"What do you want me to do about it?"* begins to help us recognize that this family lacked one of the first basic principles to growth and success: they needed to take responsibility.

Have you ever met a person who was always *about* to succeed at something, but something or someone always found a way to mess it up? It is very frustrating to see the potential in someone, (maybe even more so if that someone is you), yet never see the fulfillment of what could be, simply because this God Principle of *Taking Responsibility* is not being activated.

If you cannot learn to take responsibility for your own situation, it will most likely never change.

As a business owner for nearly 20 years, I have had many people working for me and around me. I have witnessed the destructive power of the blame game played out time and time again. From employees who made more than enough to get ahead—but never did, to business associates who did get ahead financially, but lost their marriages, their health, and their peace of mind, there has always been one inevitable constant.

Whenever anything went wrong, it was always someone or something else's fault, never their own. If you cannot first learn to take responsibility over your own situation, your own life, or the position you are in right now, then it will most likely never change. This might not be exactly what you want to hear, but if you will take hold of this, it will change your life forever. When you begin to look deeply into these verses, especially this first verse, you will notice two things from this widow woman: accusation and blame. These are the two opposites—the two *enemies*—of responsibility.

The widow cried out, *"You know* Elisha, that *your* servant feared the Lord. *You know* that he was a good man. *You know* he showed up to church every week. *You know* that he was faithful. *You know* he paid his tithes and offerings. *You know..."* Do you see the underlying accusation here? He was *your* servant. He served under *you. You know* he feared the Lord. This makes either *you* (Elisha) or God responsible for our debt. Someone's to blame. It's either *your fault*, man of God, or God's fault that we are in debt. It's *your fault* that we purchased that second donkey. It's *your fault* that we paid $150.00 a month for cable television. It's *your fault* that I went to Starbucks at least three times a week and Jack-in-the-Box, I can't even count how many times... It's *your fault*, man of God, because I was at church every week..." *What!?* Are you getting this?

Let me say it again: If you cannot learn to take responsibility for your own situation, it will most likely never change.

Former President Harry S. Truman had a sign that sat on his desk. It read: *The buck stops here!*[1] It was his way of saying, "I take responsibility. I will not blame someone else. I will make the decision. If it's wrong, I will live with the consequences. If

I'm right, I will reap the blessings." This was the president who had to make the decision to end World War II with the atomic bomb. He understood what it meant to take responsibility and to refuse to pass the blame—*"the buck"*—to someone else. It is so easy to blame. It is so easy to pass the buck. But with that said, it is my earnest desire to help you recognize, that it is also very easy to never succeed, never grow, and never obtain the levels in life that you would like to attain, all because of taking the easy route of blame and accusation.

You can blame your parents for a negative, dysfunctional up-bringing, but that will only lead to your own children blaming you for the exact same thing! Somebody has to take responsibility so the endless cycle of destruction can end and a new cycle of prosperity can begin. It might as well be you!

I have never seen a person grow from blaming others. Blaming others is like putting your vehicle in reverse. The more you blame, the farther away you get from the discoveries and potential that lay ahead. As a matter of fact, if you would treat blame like the reverse gear in a car, life would be easier and more satisfying. Blame won't let you move ahead, but if like the reverse gear, you used it only for a moment until your *front end* adjusted, and then you could throw your car into drive and once again start making progress.

You haven't been driving around in reverse have you? You'll know really quickly whether you have or not by the number of accidents, tickets, wrong turns, cricks-in-the-neck, no one-wants-to-ride-with-you, kind of problems you have.

Time and time again, people come to me with their metaphorical tickets, their accident reports, their cricks-in-their-neck problems. And guess what I hear? It's always, *someone else's fault.*

Like the widow woman, we need to recognize that the first step in breaking free from slavery and debt mindsets is to take responsibility. This is vital for heading toward spiritual development and personal growth. That means that there is no one to blame.

It is not the man of God's fault. It is not the drama in the church's fault. It is not your boss's fault. It is not your teacher's fault. It is not your mom and dad's fault. It is not the government's fault. It is not what she did to you five years ago. It is not what he did to you ten days ago. It is not even what *they* did to you yesterday. Trust me; you don't want it to be someone else's fault! If your problems and challenges really are someone else's fault, that means that someone else has control over your life. And if someone else has control over your life, that means that you don't, and you are powerless to change anything.

When you understand that the beginning of wisdom is to accept responsibility for your own problems, you will stop blaming others altogether. You will stop blaming your parents. You will stop blaming your spouse. You will stop blaming your boss. You will stop blaming the government, your background, your education or lack thereof. Because remember—what you blame, you empower. If you allow yourself to blame these uncontrollable forces for your lack of progress, you will be forever caught in a web of the past.

Don't waste another year blaming and accusing. Don't even let another day get by you. Time is precious; life is precious. Make today *your day*, your turning point. Take responsibility for where you are, who you are, and how you are. And after you have done that, you can say, *"Hello"* to endless possibilities.

I'd like to touch on something else that shows up in the conversation between Elisha and the widow woman. In that exchange, she reveals to us another flawed mentality. To understand it, I'd like to take you to another book in the Bible:

> *I appeal to you therefore, brethren, and beg of you in view of [all] the mercies of God, to make a decisive dedication of your bodies [presenting all your members and faculties] as a living sacrifice, holy (devoted, consecrated) and well pleasing to God, which is your reasonable (rational, intelligent) service and spiritual worship* (Romans 12:1 AMP).

Your *reasonable service*—this is something that the widow and her family did not understand. You see, serving or volunteering around the church each week or trying not to sin each day will not automatically activate divine *God Principles* in your life or cause you to prosper and be free of debt. She comes to Elisha and complains, but catch the underlying question, "You know, Elisha, your servant feared the Lord. You know we're faithful Christians. We served—*so why am I in debt?*"

We all need to take responsibility for what we buy and for the deals we make. We can't think that just because we've served God faithfully or have just been *good people* that everything is going to be taken care of. It doesn't work that way.

Let me break this down for you: They don't hand out medals for fulfilling your *reasonable service*. You don't get your debt canceled because you performed your *reasonable service*. It is only your reasonable service.

Serving or volunteering around the church each week and trying not to sin each day will not automatically activate *God Principles* in your life.

Don't misunderstand me. There is a reward for reasonable service after salvation one day because of our reasonable service and continued faith, God is going to say, *"Well done, good and faithful servant."* And that's a great reward—the greatest reward anyone could ever achieve. However, reasonable service doesn't automatically unlock the *God Principles* in your life and cause you to be successful in everything you do.

You see, there is a very dangerous spirit (mentality) that has been released into our world, and I see it big time in Western culture. It has infected people's minds and has caused entire generations to grow up with a warped mentality that says, *Somehow it is our right to be blessed. It's our right! Whether we press in to the things of God or not, whether we seek out and apply His principles or not, it's our right to be blessed.*

You know what I am talking about. It's the, "they owe it to us" mentality. *My parents owe it to me. My job owes it to me. The government owes it to me.* What is really sad is that this flawed thinking gets carried right into Christianity and Christians start acting like God is obligated to bless them with abundant blessings—including debt cancellation—just because they go to church on Sundays and try our best not to sin. Well I have to tell you, it just doesn't work that way.

Blame will not get you where you want to go in life. A *they owe me* attitude won't, either. This God Principle of *Taking Responsibility* will get you further, faster than you can imagine.

Let me tell you why. When you accept responsibility for your life and your situation, you not only take back control of your life, you literally free yourself to move into a bigger, brighter future of your own choosing.

Now that doesn't mean that you can change or fix everything that happened to you before today. *Taking Responsibility* is a decision to take charge from this moment forward, starting *right now.* I don't know about you, but I personally refuse to let my history control my destiny. When I accept responsibility for my past, I get to accept responsibility for my future successes as well.

**Refuse to let your history
control your destiny!**

Now, you might be reading this and think, *Wait a minute, you don't know me. You don't understand the things that have happened to me. You don't understand what I've been through. I didn't choose for certain things to happen to me.*

Do you know what my response would be? I'd look you straight in the eye and tell you, "You're absolutely right!"

There are a lot of things that happened to you that you did not choose. There are a lot of things that have happened to me that I did not choose. There are hardships, struggles, abuses, and things that happen in life that we did not want, choose, deserve, or cause, but we still own 100 percent responsibility for how we *respond* to those things.

I can promise you this: If you take responsibility for your life, your choices, and your responses, you might not like it very much at first, but you will have empowered yourself to do something about the situation. And because you have done that, your future becomes one of your own choosing and is no longer dictated by the past. You see, blaming is a declaration that says, "I'm powerless, hopeless, and unable to accomplish anything."

Taking Responsibility is a declaration that says, "I'm powerful, full of hope, and able to do anything from here on out!"

You might be thinking, *Well, this sounds good, but how do I go about doing all this? How do I stop blaming and start Taking Responsibility?* I can tell you in two words: you decide. That's the challenge. You decide that from this moment on, I will take responsibility for how I respond to the things that life or other people throw my way.

One of the ways you can activate responsibility in your life is by changing your thought life. When you realize that your decisions are governed by your thoughts, you will realize how important it is to guard your thought life.

For example, every morning I take the time to renew my mind in the Holy Spirit:

And do not be conformed to this world, but be transformed by the renewing of your mind, that you may prove what is that good and acceptable and perfect will of God (Romans 12:2).

I also remind myself of what I should think about that day:

Whatever things are true, whatever things are noble, whatever things are just, whatever things are pure, whatever things are lovely, whatever things are of good report, if there is any virtue and if there is anything praiseworthy, meditate [think] *on these things* (Philippians 4:8).

This transforms my mindset so that all my thoughts are constructive and not destructive. My renewed mind takes me to the solutions of the future and not the problems of the past.

Next, I make sure that I surround myself with people who are striving to make a difference and rarely hang out with people who live in survival mode.

Transform your mindset so that all your thoughts are *constructive* and not *destructive*.

Taking Responsibility is something you *do*. It comes about from the thoughts you think and from the choices you make. *Taking Responsibility* also means taking it upon yourself to study God's Word (the Bible) and other positive resources which enable you to gather wisdom so you can understand the difference between God's divine principles and the traditions of people and culture.

It's true that if it had not been for a miracle, this widow's family was headed for bondage and certain demise. But even within the happenings of this miracle we find several keys—several divine *God Principles* unveiled by Elisha that completely transform their lives and their future. When you begin to understand this story, you understand that the miracle did not happen until the keys started to be used, which brings me to another point.

So many people never do anything to improve their situation because they spend their whole lives waiting for a lucky break. I live in Las Vegas, and I see a lot of that around here. I know that there is a tiny percentage that you could win. But do you really think they've built all these multibillion dollar hotel/casino's off of winners? There are millions of people putting another dollar and another dollar and another dollar down on a chance to win big because they are convinced that their lives cannot change without a huge miracle (a lucky break).

Let me tell you something here: it is not God's plan for people to sit around and wait for a miracle. He doesn't want you wasting day after day waiting for something to happen, waiting for that lucky break. It is God's plan for all people to connect to Him. It's God's plan for people to find salvation through the shed blood of Jesus on the Cross. It's God's plan for you to live an overcoming life by applying *God Principles* to everything you do.

Yes, He is still in the miracle-working business, but maybe your miracle is reading this book and learning and applying the *God Principles* you need to take responsibility and change your life. You see, it's *God Principles* that progress you through life. Each challenge and each struggle gives you the opportunity to pick up things you need along the way to become the person God has called you to be.

In the story of Elisha and the widow, Elisha did not just fix the widow's problem outright. He helped her *all right*, but he did it by giving her keys—divine *God Principles*—that let her unlock the solutions to her dilemma. Even though it was not his responsibility (or his fault or his problem), he stepped in and showed her how to activate the *God Principles* in her life. The widow's miracle didn't happen until she started using the keys Elisha was showing her.

Taking Responsibility was the first key. Elisha says something very interesting, "Tell me, what you have in your house?" Through this question, Elisha helped the widow woman to stop looking outside of herself so she would stop blaming others for her situation. Instead, he helped her change her perspective by starting to look within so she could take responsibility for her predicament. "What do you have in your house?" he asked. Her answer, "Nothing but a jar of oil," was the beginning point of her miracle.

And the miracle didn't happen because it was *magic* oil or *special* oil. No. It was just what she had in hand—oil—which was the first step in responding to the God Principle of *Taking Responsibility*. This started to change her mindset and unlock the potential of multiplication and abundance. Try it for yourself. You will be surprised what you can accomplish when you get your focus right.

Check for yourself. What do you have in *your* house? This is really important because you need to understand that you already possess something that God can use and grow right now. There is something in your house. It's either in your physical house or in your spiritual house, but trust me, it's there.

You have something right now that God can take and grow to an unbelievable level, because little is much when God is in it.

And when you take responsibility for what you already have under your roof, in your hand, under your control, you give God something to work with.

Now before we move on, I want to warn those who might look within and fall prey to a drastic mistake that many make.

This is what happens: people will many times stop blaming others, but then start blaming themselves. I have seen this happen over and over again with different people. They stop blaming others, but instead of then *Taking Responsibility*, they start blaming themselves. Blaming yourself is *not Taking Responsibility!* These are two totally different things.

For someone who is in this mode or is slipping into this mode, a real wake-up call is needed, so let me just say this as "straight-up" as I can. Blaming yourself is a cop-out! And many times I've seen people use this cop-out to create a cocoon of selfishness.

Most of the time when we take responsibility for our lives or for our current state of mind or position, we have to face some tough questions. We have to confess some mistakes. We have to accept some wrong reactions and wrong turns that we've made along the way. And in these moments of *Taking Responsibility*, in these moments of taking a few deep breaths of, "OK, I've got some work to do here," we will many times experience the temptation to continue blaming, but this time the blame gets switched from someone else to ourselves.

Blaming yourself is to reject responsibility and live within a cop-out mode that is absolutely fruitless and powerless.

It is in this time of transition, of *Taking Responsibility*, that whispering voices—negative thoughts—will try to sway us into a belief that, "You're a failure, you're a screw-up, you'll never get past this, you'll never change…." Yet to give in to these voices (thoughts) and begin to blame ourselves is to reject responsibility altogether, and to live within a cop-out mode that is absolutely fruitless and powerless.

This decision causes people to live out their lives in an unproductive land, never growing, never moving forward, never making progress. And as horrible as this all sounds, people who choose this path live within a realm that seems to bring them some kind of warped sense of security, because once again they have created a cocoon of selfishness!

Now of course, people caught up in this cop-out would not see it this way (at least not at first if you were to discuss this with them), because it's such a self-absorbed limited perspective mindset that they've accepted. However, it is extremely selfish and here's the reason why: it cheats everyone around them of enjoying the fulfillment of who and what they could be and do if only they would take responsibility!

Taking Responsibility means: *I intend to do something about it.* While blaming self (living in cop-out mode) means: *I have no intentions of changing anything, and everyone around me will have to just suffer the consequences!*

What do you have in your house? She didn't have much— just a little oil. But Elisha started instructing her. "I want you to do this. I want you to do that. Go borrow vessels from the neighbors—don't get a few, get a lot. And when you come in, shut the door. Then you can start pouring." And when she did all these things, the oil flowed and her miracle began.

Endnote

1. President Harry S. Truman (May 1884–December 1972), "'The Buck Stops Here' Desk Sign"; http://trumanlibrary. org/buckstop.htm; accessed August 22, 2011.

Chapter 3

GATHER NOT A FEW

For this next *God Principle*, let's stay with the story of the prophet Elisha and the widow woman. Elisha was helping the widow woman move from a place of blame and accusation—*he was your servant, Elisha, so these problems must be your fault*—to a place of *Taking Responsibility* for her own situation. Let's look again at the first two verses of her story:

> *A certain woman of the wives of the sons of the prophets cried out to Elisha, saying, "Your servant my husband is dead, and you know that your servant feared the Lord. And the creditor is coming to take my two sons to be his slaves." So Elisha said to her, "What shall I do for you? Tell me, what do you have in the house?" And she said, "Your maidservant has nothing in the house but a jar of oil"* (2 Kings 4:1-2).

What do you have in your house? What an amazing question! I'm sure it took the widow woman by surprise. All she sees is loss. Her husband is dead, the bills are piling up, and her children are about to be sold into slavery—and here is the prophet asking her what she has in her house! What was he thinking asking her a question like that?

Elisha was introducing this woman to a very important key—the next step in bridging the gap between *Taking Responsibility* and the next *God Principle*. But first he needed to help her complete what she had started. She needed to really get the *God Principle* of *Taking Responsibility* integrated into her thinking and her life.

When people shift their responsibility onto others, they are looking outward. They are making someone out there responsible for not only the problem, but also for the solution.

**What do you have
in your house?**

Elisha's question short-circuits that process. *What do you have in your house?* The question makes her stop and think; and to get the answer, she now has to look inward to find her solution and fix her problem.

She had to stop, think, and take inventory. *What do I have in my house?* I'm sure she was puzzled. What did that have to do with anything? *Your maidservant has nothing in the house but a jar of oil. Here's the truth:* Even if it's just a simple little jar of oil, little is much when God is in it.

Little is much when your perspective changes. Little is much when you are willing to cooperate with God and His principles. With your cooperation, God can do in a moment what you couldn't do in a lifetime! When your perspective changes and you begin to embrace the solutions that are found within the endless treasures of the Scriptures, *God Principles*, your life will start to miraculously transform, even if all you have to offer is "a little jar of oil."

Now, there are two things I want you to think about here. The first is this: in and of itself, the jar of oil was nothing special. If all she had had in her house was a jar of mayonnaise, God would have used it. If all she had had in her house was a sack of potatoes, God would have used it. It's not the *thing* that you have that impresses God and changes the situation. It is your perspective and participation in the process; it's the fact that you give God something He can work with that makes all the difference in the world.

Which leads me to the second thing I want you to know: no matter what it is you need, you have something that God can work with. Right now, you have something in your house that God can use to take you from a place of lack, fear, and blame to a place of abundance, confidence, and personal responsibility.

It may be something in your physical house; it may be something in your spiritual house. But trust me, you have something right now that God can use, expand, and grow if you will begin this process of embracing these principles.

Whatever it is that you need in your life, stop and ask yourself, *What do I have right now that God can start working with? What can I do right now? What difference can I make right now?* Not in five years when the economy is better; not in ten years when the kids are older; not way down the road when you've saved up enough. What do you have in your house right now? Don't think that God has to get everything lined up so that five years down the road He can finally bless you; no way! Even though the blessings might increase from year to year or take time to completely unfold, there is something God can do with you right now if you will let Him.

Getting back to our widow woman, once Elisha helped her get her eyes off of others, he began to unlock our next God Principle, *Gathering the Ability.* Let's take a look at verse 3:

> *Then he said, "Go, borrow vessels from everywhere, from all your neighbors—empty vessels; do not gather just a few"* (2 Kings 4:3).

When I first started looking at these Scriptures and before this all started opening up to me, I really struggled with this verse. Here we have a widow woman whose husband has just died and has left the family in so much debt that their two sons are just about to go into forced labor to work off this debt, yet Elisha tells her to *"go borrow"*?

Wait a minute. That can't be right! Isn't borrowing what got this family in the mess they're in to begin with? Isn't that why they're in tremendous debt? What does Elisha mean by *"go borrow"?* That can't be right, can it? Common sense aside, the Bible teaches us with Scripture after Scripture that God doesn't want us to be the borrower; He wants us to be the lender (see Deut. 15:6, 28:12; Prov. 22:7; Rom. 13:8). So what's happening here?

Learn to borrow the *ability* to make the money

As I read and reread this passage, God began to show me something I had never seen before. Elisha is about to teach the widow woman something pretty amazing. He puts into practice the very key we just looked at; he shows her how to use something she had at hand *right now*—the skill of borrowing—in a whole new way. And in the process, he completely transformed her mindset. Instead of going out to borrow money *again*, instead of going out to borrow bread *again*, instead of going out to borrow things *again* (which would only get her further into debt), this time he taught her to borrow *the ability* to make the money, *the ability* to buy the bread, *the ability* to buy the things the family needed.

"Go," he tells her, *"borrow vessels from everywhere, from all your neighbors…"* Those were his words, but this was his message: *Lady, I'm about to use a process that you're familiar with—borrowing! But instead of doing it your way, I'm going to redeem this process for you, and in doing that, I'm going to completely change your perspective, your purpose, your mindset, and your outcome by Gathering the Ability! Are you ready?* Ready or not, that was the instruction, so that's what she did.

We can read the widow woman's story from beginning to end. It's all there in black and white so we know what's going to happen. However, can you imagine what it must have been like for her? Did she walk away scratching her head and thinking, *Empty vessels? You mean, like, pots and buckets and things? I don't get it. This man of God is strange!* But what did she have to lose? So she did it anyway, and the rest, as they say, is history.

Faith will always play an important role in the releasing and activating of *God Principles*.

Everything Elisha instructed the widow woman to do required faith, lots of faith. But she did it all anyway. You see, faith will always play an important role in the releasing and activating of *God Principles*. The Bible says, *"without faith it is impossible to please God"* (Heb. 11:6). What I'm saying is that without faith, you will never see *God Principles* activated and working in full force on your behalf.

Most people have this misconception that God is moved by *human need*. Therefore, they constantly present their *needs* to the Lord with the hopes that He'll be stirred with compassion and respond. However, let me submit to you that God is not moved by human need! If He were, places like Haiti and India would quickly become the wealthiest and most blessed countries in the world because of the immense human needs.[1]

Now don't get me wrong, I am not for a moment indicating that God is not compassionate or concerned with our well-being. Quite the contrary, for it was out of His great compassion that He wrapped Himself in human flesh and laid down His life as a sacrifice to redeem us all from the curse of sin and rescue humankind from certain destruction. However, when a human need arises, God seldom fixes the problem outright. Instead, He provides divine laws and Kingdom principles that, when embraced and practiced on a consistent basis, fix the problem at hand every time!

Heaven is not moved by human need; it's moved by human faith. *Faith is the currency of Heaven!* And it is divine laws and Kingdom principles that govern the storehouses where the blessings abide and where faith makes its purchases!

God does not respond to your needs. He responds to your faith. So it is probably not going to surprise you that one of the keys to making this or any of the *God Principles* work is for you to inject faith into it. Just try it and watch them begin to work on your behalf.

Heaven is not moved by human need; it's moved by human faith. Faith is the currency of Heaven!

Our widow woman, regardless of how crazy she may have thought Elisha's instructions were at the moment, followed them to a T. Just picture it.

Her next door neighbor is at the sink washing dishes. She looks out her kitchen window and says, *"Oh, no! Here she comes again—the borrower!"* She yells to the kids, "Kids! Quick! Turn off the TV! Close the blinds! Everyone be real quiet! Maybe she'll think we're not home!"

But as the kids jump up to turn off the television, the Borrower is already knocking. *Nooo!* Her neighbor thinks, *I wonder what she wants this time!*

Can you imagine the look of surprise and bewilderment on her neighbor's face when the widow woman asks if she can borrow a couple of empty pots?

"Excuse me?" her neighbor sputters as the questions begin to turn in her head, *You want what? You don't want my last loaf of bread, again? You don't want a couple of bucks, again? You don't want to borrow a cup of sugar, again? You want empty pots?*

"What?" she questions again. "Empty pots? Well, yeah, sure. Come on in. Sit down. Put your feet up. Kids, kids, come help me. Our friend here needs to borrow some pots. You grab the stuff in the kitchen; I'll go check in the garage. Are you sure that's all you need?"

Let me interrupt this scene and tell you something: you will be amazed at how much people will suddenly want to help you when you ask to borrow *the ability* instead of *the source.*

I know for me personally, I never get excited when people come and want to borrow money from me, but I do get excited when they come to me and say, "Hey, would you talk to me about how you started your different businesses?" or, "Can you talk to me about what it was like to start a church with just six people? How did you do it? What were your challenges?"

"Yes, yes, come on in. Sit down!" I'll tell them. "I'll even buy the lunch. Just sit down and listen."

I've said "no" to people asking to borrow money—you probably have, too—but I have never turned someone away who asked to borrow some of the wisdom that I have gathered. In fact, I like it! It's exciting to help people who want to help themselves.

As I mentioned earlier in the book, I live in Las Vegas, Nevada, and in these days and in this economy, it is not an uncommon thing to see people standing along the side of the road with a cardboard sign: *"Will work for Food."* I don't mean to appear harsh or cold-hearted, but I have to tell you, it doesn't move me very much. The other day I was stopped at a red light and this guy pops up—Windex in one hand, paper towels in the other. "Hey, Mister, I'll wash your windows for a quarter."

I said, "Do it, man. Let's go!" I like that. I like it when people are *doing* something. I like it when I see people out gathering. I wish I saw more of it happening. It pains me to say this, but we have become a nation of handouts and freebies.

We've become a *"what can I get for nothing"* culture. So many people in this country walk around with a *"you-owe-it-to-me"*-shaped chip on their shoulder. We've mastered the art of borrowing, all right. We've mastered the art of borrowing the source, when what we need to do is become masters at borrowing the ability and gathering wisdom. I believe more people would do just that if they knew where to begin. So with that in mind, I want to give them a place to begin.

**Stop gathering useless information
and become a *careful gatherer*.**

First let me start with a warning. Let me tell you what and where not to gather. America has become a nation of gatherers—gatherers of tons of useless information from television, Internet, music, and so forth. People spend much of their time gathering useless information and then wonder why they can't seem to get ahead in life. Even the Bible addresses this need to gather the ability or gather wisdom with a direct statement, *"My people are destroyed for lack of knowledge"* (Hosea 4:6). That statement is as true today as the day it was written.

Become a careful gatherer. Take the time to look at what it is you are gathering. If your goal is to gather wisdom and to gather the ability to better your life, how much of what you need are you going to find reading magazines or watching soap operas? How much of the information that you need to move you forward in mind, body, and spirit will you find listening to the same old music that you've been listening to for 20 years?

Everyone enjoys an old love song here and there, but listening for hours and hours to the same music every day is a waste, especially when you could spend most of those same hours *Gathering the Ability,* or gathering wisdom, by listening to CDs on leadership, investing, communication, and so forth. For your own sake, please consider what it is you are gathering because, whether you realize it or not, those things, those thoughts and ideas, those beliefs and concepts, are the raw material from which you will build your future.

It is imperative that you stop and consider and then be selective regarding both what, and from whom, you borrow. And when you do go gathering, rather than gathering the source, go gather the ability and the know-how to *do* something; go gather the knowledge you need to change your situation.

You may be thinking, *This sounds great, but how do I do that? Where do I start?* Start with people around you. Find people who have been through the storms of life, through rough transitions, through hardships and disappointments, and have come out the other side still standing. If you look for them, you will find them. Find the pioneers in your field of interest; find people who have started businesses from nothing, who saved up a couple thousand dollars and worked until they had success. These are the people you want to borrow information from; these are the folks who have the wisdom you need. Where are these people? Look around you. They are everywhere.

I pastor an amazing church that is very diversified in ethnicity and abilities. In our group we have supervisors and managers, as well as many business owners and entrepreneurs; we have published authors and accomplished musicians; we have a board member of a bank, several gifted teachers, and even a teacher of teachers. We have people in our congregation who know how to fix things, crafts people from different trades who are highly skilled at what they do (like the lady who edited this book and made me look a lot smarter than I really am).

We have a very diverse, multicultural church, so there are many people among us who have moved from one country to another and who have faced major challenges of language, culture, and acclamation. Can you imagine all that could be gathered from these individuals? This is one of the great perks of connecting and getting involved with a church. Not only do you end up with a very large extended family, but it opens the door to meet various types of people from whom you can gather while at the same time blessing them in some way as well. The main thing is that you just go out there and look for people.

Reposition yourself to meet people and obtain opportunities. I doubt very many opportunities will come knocking at your door while you sit there watching television. Instead, get out there and start saying, "Hi!" to people while you take a walk. Strike up a friendly conversation with a neighbor. Find someone who is successful at doing something that you want to do or who has mastered something you need to know. And when you find them, introduce yourself and say, "Hey, I admire what you've done! Can I buy you a cup of coffee and just pick your brain for an hour or so. I'm trying to increase in that area myself." Or, "Could I buy you lunch and talk to you about how you did this or that." Then, when you take them to coffee or to lunch, spend the hour mostly listening. It's important to ask some good quality questions, but spend most of the time listening and taking notes. By the way, did I mention that you should *listen?* I emphasize *listening* because, in general, people have a bad habit of talking too much. It's very hard to gather from someone while you're talking.

I remember being in one of these little "gathering sessions" a while back, but I was not the gatherer. I was the one who had been asked to lunch to share with this individual what I had learned in a certain area. I was absolutely amazed as I sat there and listened to this person talk for 15, 30, 45 minutes, not even asking a single question that was remotely related to why we were there. I was convinced that this would have gone on the entire time, so in my desire to see this person grow and develop, I finally interrupted and reminded that person why we were there.

Remember, most of the people you want to gather from are probably busy people. Make the time count! Be attentive and listen! Gather as much wisdom as you can. Don't treat that lunch like you're hanging out with one of your friends. You're there to gather. Let them do most of the talking, and you will be amazed at what you can learn. Now I realize that not everyone will be able to go to lunch with you. Like I said, most successful people are busy people—that's part of the reason they are successful. So when you do get some time with them, gather, gather, and gather some more. Gather all the ability-wisdom you can!

At the same time, you don't have to wait for those busy people to work you in before you can grow and learn. The majority of your gathering could be done through another group of people—those who have gone on before you, but who have taken the time to write down the wisdom of their lifetime and leave that legacy in a book. Engineers, ministers, poets, war heroes, inventors, financiers, presidents, kings—there are people from every walk of life, people who have lived through every type of experience who have taken the time to write their story and leave it behind for you and me to read and utilize.

There are people who have written down *God Principles* and amazing keys that unlock the complexities of life and have put their revelations and experiences and ideas in books so you could shortcut your own learning curve by standing on the shoulders of their wisdom.

Spiritual Life

Celebration of Discipline — Richard Foster
The Applause of Heaven — Max Lucado
Screw Tape Letters — C.S. Lewis
Right People Right Place Right Plan — Jentezen Franklin
Too Busy Not to Pray — Bill Hybels
Purpose Driven Life — Rick Warren

Leadership

Developing the Leader within You — John C. Maxwell
Lincoln on Leadership — Don Phillips
Spiritual Leadership — J. Oswald Sanders
The 21 Irrefutable Laws of Leadership — John C. Maxwell
Jack: Straight from the Gut — Jack Welch

Marriage — Family

His Needs—Her Needs — Willard Harley
If Only He Knew — Gary Smalley
Building Your Mate's Self-esteem — Dennis & Barbara Rainey
Parenting Isn't for Cowards — James Dobson
Love Talk — Les & Leslie Parrott

Personal Growth & Development

Today Matters — John C. Maxwell
The Seasons of Life — Jim Rohn
7 Habits of Highly Effective People — Stephen Covey
How to Win Friends & Influence People — Dale Carnegie
Search for Significance — Robert McGee

I've heard it said, that people who read, lead. I don't necessarily agree with that statement. You see, it depends on what you're reading and how you apply what you read, as well as how much you act upon what you've learned. However, if you are reading—gathering—from the right sources and you're prepared to act upon this new knowledge, then yes, you will begin to lead!

**Go gather an idea, a concept,
or a perspective; go borrow
a principle or a revelation.**

Go to your local library. They are free, and they are filled with vessels, "empty pots" just waiting for someone to come in and borrow. Go gather an idea, a concept, or a perspective; go borrow a principle or a revelation that God gave to people who took the time to release it in books so others could glean from their wisdom.

Go read the Bible. It's filled with letters from God which contain information that can absolutely change your life, your family, and your future.

There are many different ways to gather ability and to borrow wisdom. I would like to introduce to you a resource that you may not have considered. It's something I borrowed from a brilliant gatherer: your own personal Board of Directors.[2] Now, you may be reading this and thinking, *You're telling me I need my own Board of Directors? What are you talking about?* You heard me right. Everyone should have their own personal Board of Directors (just don't tell them they are on your Board, that way you don't have to pay them).

Let me tell you who you should have on your Board. If you are raising small children, you should have someone on your Board who has raised children that you think are very good adults now. If you are starting a business, you should have someone on your Board who has not only started a business, but who has been very successful with it. Whatever it is that you want or need to know, learn, or be, find people who are successful in that arena so you can pull and borrow and gather from their wisdom, their choices, their abilities, and their experiences.

I can hear you thinking, *Good heavens! What have I been doing all these years? I have to get myself a Board of Directors!* Yes, you do. And as you build and grow and expand, you will need to periodically adjust your personal Board so you can continue to learn and grow and prosper and so you can make good decisions and become everything that you are destined to be. And since these individuals don't know that they're on your board, you can easily make changes along the way without any issues. If you're the biggest person in your circle (if everyone looks up to you), your circle is too small! You must expand and get people around you (Board members) whom you admire or look up to in some way.

This might sound strange, but you should have some people around you who intimidate you! I mean this in a positive way. Not intimidating in a fearful or negative way, but rather in a way where you know that if you try to give up they will kick you in the backside! It's important to have some positive intimidation around you so that you know good and well that if you start whining and complaining, these people will not let you get away with it, but instead will let you have it!

You must also remember when choosing Board members that people's financial status doesn't determine their level of wisdom in all areas. In other words, you might have more money than the guy next door, but he might be able to teach you a whole lot about gardening.

There is so much to be gathered from those around you. Don't wait another day, start your *new* kind of borrowing today, and just watch things begin to change for you.

Now let's go back to the story of our widow woman for a minute. Not only is she amazed by how different the neighbors are now acting toward her since she's obtained this new perspective, but it seems that they are really excited about helping her with this new task of gathering.

It's also important to highlight from this text the last few words of the instructions she received. It's not enough that Elisha the prophet has the poor woman out borrowing empty vessels from all her neighbors, he also gives her a very specific command. Take a look at the last few words of that verse: *do not gather just a few.*

There is a wisdom key hidden within this *God Principle*, and it is this: when you gather, gather lavishly. We know from reading on to the end of her story that the oil ceased when the widow woman ran out of places to pour it. I wonder if she realized what all she stood to gain by following Elisha's instructions full out? You see, she could have chosen not to— she could have gone out and gathered just a few empty vessels, but this would have been disastrous.

When you gather, gather lavishly.

If the widow woman had chosen to live with a survival mode mentality, gathering just enough to "get by," her story would have ended in tragedy. Living in survival mode is extremely dangerous. It will keep you trapped in a poverty mindset, and it will keep your dreams, your vision, your expectations, your plans, and your life *small*. Stay out of it!

Another trap you will want to avoid is what I call the "Lucky Break" mentality. People with this mindset don't even bother to gather. They live out their lives believing for that one big pay day—a lucky break, a miracle moment. Do miracles still happen today? Yes, they do! But please realize that it is not by accident that the size of the widow woman's miracle was directly linked to her effort and her ability in gathering. Part of God's plan is for you to participate in your life. People who wait for a lucky break spend their lives *waiting*. God doesn't want you to wait. He wants you to live. He wants you to act!

So, if you have been waiting for that one lucky break, stop it! Go out and start *Gathering the Ability* to not only sustain yourself, but to prosper and grow whether that lucky break ever happens or not. Start applying *God Principles* in your life. Then start injecting faith into those principles. You will be amazed at the transformation that will start happening!

If you keep pressing in, if you keep applying *God Principles*, it will be only a matter of time before the oil starts to flow in your life. Make sure you're prepared to handle it when it starts. Many times the reason people are not blessed abundantly is simply because they are not *prepared to be blessed* abundantly. Make sure that you have gathered *"not a few"* but lavishly, so you'll be ready for an abundant flow.

Endnotes

1. "Haiti & India, Poverty Levels"; http://www.compassion. com/poverty/poverty-map.htm.

2. Andy Andrews, *Secret Board of Directors: Mastering the 7 Decisions that Determine Personal Success* (Nashville: Thomas Nelson, 2008).

Chapter 4

SHUT THE DOOR BEHIND YOU

In this chapter, I'm going to release to you the single most important action that you can take to become effective in everything that you do. The key is to be consistent at this principle in order to become an effective husband or wife, an effective parent, an effective business person, an effective Christian, or just effective in general.

This principle will affect you spiritually, physically, emotionally, relationally, and financially, and it will unlock the doors to joyous living and a genuinely happy demeanor.

The *Principle of Forgiveness* is now being recognized in many fields—not just in religious circles—but in the medical field, in the psychiatric field, in health and nutrition, and many others.

**The key is to be consistent
in order to become effective.**

Many people have wrongly assumed that *forgiveness* is a religious term, period. However, the fact of the matter is that forgiveness is much, much more than that! Even though it's misunderstood and misrepresented, forgiveness is something that personally affects every one of us whether we realize it or not.

With that said, I'm sure you've already figured it out. The single most important act you can do each day to cause you to be effective in everything you do is: *forgive.*

When you learn to greet each day with a forgiving spirit, you activate one of the most life-changing *God Principles* ever given!

> *Let all bitterness, wrath, anger, turmoil, and evil speaking* [which would include gossip, talking bad about people, speaking negative, etc.] *be put away from you. And be kind to one another, tenderhearted, forgiving one another, even as God in Christ forgave you* (Ephesians 4:31-32).

Maybe the reason we have been told to *be kind one to another* is because it impacts us, and not just them—or the one we're being kind to. So many times we think that doing the right thing is all about blessing others or helping others, when indeed and in fact, many times the one who is impacted the most is us!

Be kind one to another. "Man, I really like your shoes." or "You have a wonderful smile." The compliments may be pointed toward them, but what is it actually doing in you?

If you don't look carefully, you just might miss this principle in our widow woman's story, but it's there. After getting her to *Take Responsibility* and then after sending her out to *Gather the Ability*, the old prophet drops in a very interesting instruction. Let's look at verse 4 again and see if you can spot it.

And when you have come in, you shall shut the door behind you and your sons; then pour it into all those vessels, and set aside the full ones (2 Kings 4:4).

Is it just me, or does Elisha seems to get a little over-instructive in this verse? *"When you go in your house, shut the door behind you...."* When I first read this passage I thought, *This seems like a little bit more information than you'd usually give to an adult.*

Now I can understand him saying, *"Close the door behind you,"* if he were speaking to a child because, of course, up to a certain age all children believe that the best position for a door to be in is open (or is that just the case in my house?). But it's a very strange sentence to say to the adult of the house. It's a very strange sentence to say to the one who's *paying the power bill.* "I want you to go in and close the door behind you."

That's like me calling my wife and saying, "Honey, you're probably going to beat me home from work tonight, but I'll swing by and pick you up in a little while and we'll go grab a bite for dinner. Oh, by the way, when you go in the house—remember to *close the door* behind yourself, dear." That just seems like a little bit too much—don't you think?

After reading this verse a few times, I immediately realized that this had to be a reference to a greater principle. Elisha wasn't just giving her a friendly reminder to close the physical door on her own house and save on the power bill. But rather, through this statement, he was about to teach her, and us, how to activate the flow of the oil. Are you ready? Elisha said, *"Shut the door behind you..."* and then pour the oil into the vessels.

As I began to pray and meditate on these Scriptures, the Lord spoke to me and said, "The oil never flows freely until the door to the past is securely closed."

Every time you close the door to the past, a spiritual door opens, which usually creates an opportunity in the natural. Unfortunately it works vice versa as well. Every time we open the door to the past, a spiritual door closes just the same in front of us.

Close the door and the oil will flow. Close the door and God's spirit will begin to flow in your life.

Close the door and the oil will flow. Or in other words: close the door and God's Spirit will begin to flow in your life. When God's Spirit begins to flow in your life, you become more productive, more positive, and more effective. Close the door, and you will begin to increase. Close the door, and you'll become more efficient and joyful in everything that you do. Close the door and your future will become even more beautiful than you could have ever imagined. *Closing the Door* activates three or four *God Principles* in our lives automatically, but we're going to focus on this one for the moment.

This is the area in many people's lives, the very spot where the *flow* or the *fulfillment* of what God has planned for us stops! This is where many people stall out in their progress and forfeit their greatest potential. Over and over I have seen talented, gifted, wonderful people head into a circling pattern simply because they will not "let it go."

"Close the door behind you," is the *Principle of Forgiveness*; it is the principle of letting it go. Let it go, close the door, forgive. This is the single most important action that you can take each day which will enable you to become effective in everything that you do. You see, many people don't recognize the power of forgiveness or the strength of forgiveness.

And many people have the misconception that forgiveness is only a spiritual act that keeps our hearts right before God (which indeed it is and indeed it does), but it is so much more than that. The principle and power of forgiveness is much more inclusive and much more far-reaching than many may have ever considered. Forgiveness is not simply a

Christian duty. Forgiveness is a divine law and a God principle, and when such a law or principle is practiced, it empowers, it enlightens, and it advances the individual or the cause every single time.

Despite popular belief, forgiveness is not a gift that you give someone else. Forgiveness is a gift that you give yourself. Many today look at forgiveness as something that you withhold and that you only bestow on those who have become worthy or deserving by crawling humbly into your presence with remorse and repentance so that you will somehow allow them to continue living by releasing the dreadful debilitating spell that you hold over them.

Forgiveness is not a gift that you give someone else. Forgiveness is a gift that you give yourself.

When the truth of the matter is that you are the one under the spell. You are the one under the curse, and you are the one who is going to get liberated and empowered and enlightened by speaking forgiveness. You have it all backward. If you keep waiting for the one who hurt you to deserve your forgiveness, you just might end up waiting a lifetime. You just might end up missing out on some of the best things that God has planned for your life.

At the same time, those doors that you've been hoping will open up ahead of you—well, it's probably very unlikely to happen if you refuse to "shut the door behind you." When you shut a door to the past, a door always opens to the future. It's a God principle; it's automatic. But if you're refusing to let something go, if you're refusing to close that door behind you, you just might get to the end of your life and say, "It wasn't worth it. I'm the one who ended up suffering. I wish I would have just closed the door and let it go."

Don't allow your history to control your destiny. When you refuse to *close the door*, you are giving your past the permission to dwell in your present, which is ultimately causing you to become a slave to unforgiveness. And since slavery in any form is wrong, one could even argue that you are now willingly committing sin by holding yourself captive, simply because you refuse to fully and completely forgive. By a simple act of forgiveness, you release the demons of the past—with which you can do nothing about anyway—and you free yourself of the slavery of what was. You create within yourself a new heart, a new beginning, and a new future.

In my studies, I have found two different ways that people close the door. First, is the *partial closing*. It looks closed from a distance, but can be easily opened by a good gust of wind, which regularly happens—by the way—in the storms of life.

**Forgiveness is not an
emotion; it's a decision.**

When the storms begin to rage, that which looked closed, blows wide open and causes a real big mess! So many people live in this reality. So many people live in this spot, which is in denial, really. The door looks closed, but certainly is not latched and not even close to being locked. It only *looks* closed because they have only gone through the motions of forgiveness, but never really the true act or decision of forgiveness.

Let me speak to a specific someone who is reading this right now and whose heart rate has already started to elevate because this is all too familiar to you. May these words penetrate into your very heart and soul and may you be enlightened forever as you finally *let it go* and embrace the endless possibilities of what's ahead. It's decision time, it's time for action, and it's time to choose forgiveness so you can become everything you were created to be!

"Forgiveness is not an emotion; it's a decision."[1] When you make it an emotional thing, you only go through the motions and partially close the door, but it's still cracked open a little bit and nothing has really changed. However, when you make a decision to speak forgiveness, that's when the door closes all the way and you can proceed on your new path.

The enemy of your soul (who wants you to live in the valley of despair, anger, and regret) will come knocking to see if the door is really closed. But I encourage you to just use his testings or temptings to reopen that door as reminders and opportunities to say, "Sorry, not only is the door closed, but that person you're looking for no longer lives here; a new person with a forgiving spirit now resides at this residence."

Now of course, it's not that easy, and he doesn't give up that easily either because he really doesn't want to see you live in your newfound freedom. So many times he'll come knocking again and again, trying to get you to dig up "the stuff" that you've already let go of, but you must hold your ground and use his continual knocking as a reminder to pray for that person or situation that you've forgiven, which will make you even stronger.

I can promise you that if he sees you using his knocking as a reminder to pray for that person you forgave, the knocking will quickly stop. I can almost hear someone thinking at this moment, *I wonder if my door to past hurts, regrets, and offenses is really closed or not?* You'll find out really quickly whether you have really closed the door by watching what happens when the next storm hits. Picture this, you're going along, everything is good, you have a smile on your face, you have a song in your heart, and then the storm hits.

"What do you mean I got denied for that loan? Ahhhh! That ex of mine has messed up my credit, messed up my life. I'll never get ahead because of my ex! You'll know when the storm hits.

"What do you mean you're leaving the team? What do you mean you just 'want to be friends?' But I thought.... It's just like when I was growing up! Dad left me, everyone always leaves! My girlfriend married my best friend out of high school—everybody always ends up rejecting me and walking out! I can't trust anybody..." You'll know really quickly when the storm hits and the wind blows if indeed the door to the past is really closed or not.

Immediately people who have not fully closed the door to the past will slide right back to square one and begin to blame and accuse all over again. Eventually they will dust themselves off, take responsibility, and start all over. Slowly but surely, they start climbing back up those stairs again, climbing back up that ladder. Slowing but surely they'll start to regain ground that was lost, because when the door is open and the wind blows, it will slide you all the way back to square one.

If people have to go through this two or three times before learning, that in itself would be tough. However, many are living out this cycle over and over again—and quite frankly, it's killing them! I'm speaking to those who keep pulling themselves up by their boot straps. You start doing all the right things—*Naming* your day, *Taking Responsibility,* and *Gathering* wisdom. Then you get back to *Close the Door* and everything falls apart again.

My dear friend, it is time to break the cycle, let it go, make a decision to greet each day with a forgiving spirit from here on out, and refuse to let your history determine your destiny! You see, when the door only appears to be closed, it's kind of like living an old Chinese proverb with a twist: I buried the hatchet, but I remember where I buried it.[2] *I'm going to let it go, but don't push me, is what you're really saying. I'm going to let it go, but don't push me too far because I'm not above going and digging it back up and using it on you again.* This is really not a life worth living.

The second way is the correct way that we all want to close the door. We close it, we lock it, we throw away the key; we bury the house in a million tons of concrete and build a sky-scraper on top of it. The door is closed! It's gone. We couldn't get back to it and open it even if we tried.

Think about it, if the closing of the door releases the oil— the Spirit of God in our lives—or the flow of prosperity, then I don't want to *kind of* close it, because I don't want to *kind of* get better. If the closing of the door releases the flow or the ability to grow or succeed or progress, then I'm not going to *kind of* close the door because I don't want the oil to *kind of* flow! I'm going to absolutely close the door and get an absolute flow of the goodness of God coming into my life.

If you will greet each day with a forgiving spirit and if you will make up your mind to forgive even those who don't deserve it and those who don't ask for it, you will release to yourself one of the greatest gifts available—the gift of a pure heart and a productive mind.

The Bible says the thief (the devil) does not come except to steal, and to kill, and to destroy (see John 10:10). Unforgiveness is a thief and a robber. It will rob you of hours, days, weeks, months, and years through time wasted with angry, unproductive thoughts that you can never get back. However, what is still to come can be lived to the fullest by *Closing the Door* today and letting go of what was, letting go of the past, and speaking forgiveness.

How much further could you be as an individual; how much further could we be as a country; how much further could we be in our pursuit of godliness; how much more effective could we be where we work and in what we do to impact the world in general? How much further along would we be if many valuable hours had not been wasted plotting and imagining revenge or confrontation? When we truly forgive, we release bitterness, which leads to the contentment of the soul and productivity of the mind.

"Ah, but I just can't let it go.... You don't understand what they did to me! You don't understand how badly I was abused! You don't understand how they betrayed me—you don't understand how they back-stabbed me—how they hurt me! You don't know the words they said over and over and over again!"

You're right. I don't know—I wasn't there. But let me tell you what I do know: harboring anger and resentment toward others and not forgiving people, whether they deserve it or not, poisons your soul and limits your growth. That's what I do know!

As I speak about letting it go, I'm reminded of a story I once heard about an eagle. One day this man was out hiking in the mountains enjoying all the sights and sounds of nature. It was one of those picture perfect days, 75 degrees, crystal clear with postcard-like scenery everywhere he looked. The hiker was enjoying his adventure immensely, but never could have imagined what was about to unfold before him. As he reached the top of the mountain, he found himself a nice rock on which to rest and take in the views. Quietly he sat there overlooking the entire valley from where he had begun his journey several hours earlier. As he pulled a sandwich from his backpack, something flew overhead which instantly caught his attention. He quickly focused in on what seemed to be the largest most-impressive eagle that he had ever seen. He guesstimated the wing span of this impressive bird to be 8 or 9 feet across. *Magnificent!* He thought as he watched the eagle smoothly glide through the air.

As he continued to snack on his granola bar, he noticed the bird had entered into some kind of circling maneuver, peering down with its incredible eagle vision at the valley floor below. After five minutes or so, it seemed as if the eagle had locked on to what it was looking for and instantly threw itself into a tremendous dive. The hiker had never seen anything like this as the eagle seemed to reach speeds that appeared unrecoverable.

Quickly the man's attention turned to the ground to try to see what had caught the eagle's eye. He could barely make out something scurrying along the valley floor before *wham!* The eagle had snatched up its prey and was now pumping its majestic wings, climbing higher and higher back up to the heights from where it started.

The hiker, who was now on his feet, stood there in awe as this amazing scene unfolded before his very eyes. He watched as the eagle continued to gain altitude, clutching tightly to the little varmint it had dove down to get. After a few minutes of witnessing this amazing scene, suddenly something unexpected happened.

Without warning, without reason, the great majestic bird's flight became erratic, and *whoosh* its wings tucked into its self and the eagle started to drop out of the sky like a ball of lead.

"What just happened?! Did someone shoot it? I didn't hear a gunshot...I don't understand?" the hiker spoke to himself in a confused voice as he watched in utter amazement as this majestic creature plummeted to the ground.

A small poof of dust arose from the ground; he could almost hear the *thud* as the eagle hit the valley floor below. Amazed, bewildered, and totally confused, the hiker just couldn't figure out what had just transpired. His curiosity got the best of him so he decided he had to climb down the mountain and take a closer look.

With his adrenalin pumping, he made pretty good time getting to the valley floor. Quickly he hurried over to the area where he had seen the eagle hit the ground, and sure enough, lying face down—almost looking as if it were sleeping—there the bird lay. Even with its wings folded in, lying there on the ground, the bird still appeared quite large and a bit intimidating. At first the hiker hesitated to approach the large bird, but after remembering that it had now been laying there well over an hour, he concluded that indeed it must be dead. Nevertheless, he decided to pick up a stick and proceed with caution. Slowly he walked up to the eagle and gave it a little poke. Nothing happened, nothing moved. "What is going on?" he muttered to himself. After standing there in silence for a moment, he took the end of his stick and flipped the large bird onto its back.

What he saw next absolutely blew his mind. Still clutched tightly in the large claws of this eagle was the prey that it had dived down so powerfully to get. This eagle had dove down and snatched up a weasel. Unlike a field mouse or rabbit, weasels are fighters with very long claws—not to mention mean, mean, mean.

Just a split second before the eagle had snatched this weasel off of the ground; the weasel had instinctively flipped unto its back and prepared itself to fight. This ultimately meant that when the eagle grabbed the weasel and pulled it into its chest to start flying back upward, the weasel's teeth and claws were in position to do damage. Immediately the weasel starting fighting, clawing, and biting into the eagle's chest. As the hiker looked more closely, he could see that the eagle had held onto that weasel so long that the weasel broke through the eagle's thick chest and had torn into the eagle heart, causing instant death.

I tell this story in this particular chapter of forgiveness because it relates to the way we act so many times throughout life. You see, at any time the eagle could have let go of that weasel and not only stopped the pain, but saved its life. The eagle was in complete control of the situation. The eagle only had to *let it go*, and it would have had many productive years ahead to enjoy. Instead, it held on tightly to the thing that was killing it. It held on tightly to the one thing that was tearing into it and causing damage.

How many times do we hold on to things that are tearing us apart? How many times have we refused to let go of things which we knew—and we could feel—were causing us so much pain? It's not worth it; let it go, and let the healing process begin!

The Bible compares us to eagles many times; and with that comparison, I must say that too many eagles are dying today needlessly, simply because they will not let it go. When you refuse to forgive someone, you become the eagle who has swooped down and grabbed the consequences of holding back forgiveness. It's unproductive, it's debilitating, and quite frankly, it's deadly. Close the door. Let it go. Embrace the power of forgiveness, and just watch your life begin to flourish.

A forgiving spirit *allows* you to let go of the past and embrace a compelling new future

When you close the door, when you let it go, the oil will begin to flow in your life, and the plan of the enemy will be voided out. Dear friend, when you close the door, God steps in and takes the plans of the enemy over your life, rips them up right then and there, throws them on the floor, and says, "Now I have a plan for you!"

A forgiving spirit allows you to let go of the past and embrace a compelling new future. There is so much potential not being recognized because the door is not closed. There are so many life-changing, world-impacting futures that hang in the balance today because a decision has not yet been fully made to simply let it go. It's so simple, but it's not always so easy. Or you could say it like this: it's easy to do and it's even easier not to do.

What a tragedy it would have been for this widow woman, who really needed a miracle in her life, who really needed a miraculous change in her future to miss out because of a door left open. What a tragedy, after *Taking Responsibility* and *Gathering the Ability*—this woman on the verge of a breakthrough, on the verge of a tremendous miracle, on the verge of a life changing moment—to then void it all out, to cancel all progress up to now simply because she couldn't close the door. "I just can't do it; I just can't do it."

As I began to think about this early one morning, the thought came into my mind: *How many ministries have never been started? How many lives have not been impacted? How many businesses were never started or never succeeded simply because the door was left open?*

Did you know that there are ministries, businesses, and families that either never happened or never succeeded, and it wasn't the economy that they blamed it on—and it wasn't the streak of bad luck or the financial problems or the guy who stole from them. It wasn't that misunderstanding, even though that might have been the last straw. It wasn't all those things at all. More times than you think, it was unforgiveness and nobody even considered it a possibility.

Unforgiveness will cause a deluge of unproductive thoughts, and this plethora of unproductive thoughts will lead to bad decisions—and it only takes a few bad decisions before your vision starts to get blurred, and pretty soon you end up in a ditch of despair, and it all could have been avoided by a simple, yet not so easy, act of forgiveness.

The question most commonly asked to me regarding this matter is this, "But what if they don't ask for forgiveness?" The truth of the matter is that most of them won't. Can I just be real with you for a moment? Not only will most of them not ask for forgiveness, but believe it or not, a high percentage of them won't even know that they should. Most of the people who hurt you don't even know how much it bothered you. And while you're lying awake, planning and thinking about what you're going to say, they're home, sleeping like babies, completely unaffected. I know that just burns you up to hear me say that, but I'm hoping that the power of these words will awaken you and shake you out of your sleep, causing you to recognize that the only one who is suffering because of unforgiveness is you!

Abraham Lincoln said, "Forgiveness is a secret that is hidden in plain sight." He said, "It costs nothing, but it's worth millions. It's available to all, but used by few. And if you harness the power of forgiveness you will be sought after and regarded highly and not coincidentally, you will also be forgiven by others."[3]

That is powerful! President Lincoln was a man who lived and understood the *Principle of Forgiveness.*

Our history books have been greatly altered to make us Americans look like a much more friendly, loving nation that rallied around our great, fearless president—the 16th president of the United States—but the truth is very different. President Lincoln was hated and eventually assassinated. He was hated for some of the things he stood for. He was rejected, criticized, talked down to by most of Washington's elite. Almost every move he made was scorned and criticized publicly. Even his personal appearance and looks were openly attacked.

He was commonly referred to as gawky, unrefined, a buffoon: *Abe-the-Ape.* The elite referred to him as "a stupid country lawyer" who didn't know how to dress himself. He was very tall and lanky with long arms and legs and had trouble finding clothes that fit him. Yet he was the very one who said, "I will greet each day with a forgiving spirit."

At the end of the Civil War, the nation was divided; people were hurting. Family members had to fight against family members. It was an awful time in our history. And finally there was a peace agreement—a settlement. The Civil War was over and the defeated generals had agreed to meet at a designated place to come up on a platform and sign the peace treaty.

When they arrived, there was President Abraham Lincoln and the victorious general lined up on the other side of the stage. History records that as the defeated generals began to come up the steps of the stage, people began to boo and hiss. Without hesitation, President Lincoln stood up and quieted the crowd. What he did next shocked everyone.

He snapped to attention and raised his hand to his head and saluted the defeated and demoralized generals. One by one, all of the victorious generals stood up and snapped to attention and saluted the losing generals as they marched up on the stage.

People criticized it. "I can't believe it. They stood for the wrong things." However, to his critics, President Lincoln responded like this, "This nation is divided and the best thing we can do to get us back together is to show a spirit of forgiveness. My actions to salute the opposing generals, was my first act of forgiveness."[4]

Yet even as admirable as President Lincoln seemed to be, I cannot go any further without speaking of the greatest example of all—the man, who was perfect and never hurt anyone.

Instead, He restored sight to the blind; He restored hearing to the deaf, and voice to the mute. He even restored life to several who had died. He was a man of compassion who openly fed the multitudes and put others first, a man who lived to serve—a man who lived to bless, a man who lived to die.

Not an ordinary man, but rather God wrapped in human flesh; He left all His majesty, left a place where He was adored and worshiped 24/7 to come to a place where He was persecuted, spit on, and mocked. This same Man was wrongfully accused—beaten with many stripes nearly to death. Abused by the soldiers, rejected by His peers, He hung on a cross with 9-inch spikes through His wrists and a 12-inch spike through both feet. Exhausted and thirsty, blood poured down His face from a crown of thorns that had been mockingly shoved down into His brow. He was the only Man who ever hung on a cross who actually had the power at any moment to call on millions of angels to come and wipe out anyone who opposed Him. Yet instead—in great agony—He opened His mouth and cried out, *"Father, forgive them for they know not what they do"* (Luke 23:34 KJV).

What most people fail to see is that these words were activating the same *God Principles* that we're talking about in this chapter. Jesus called out, *"Father, forgive them...."* I believe He was also saying, "Close the door so the oil can flow." And the Bible teaches that not many days after that, they were all gathered together in one accord, in one place, and suddenly there came a sound from Heaven as a rushing mighty wind—it filled the house where they were sitting, and they were all filled with the Holy Spirit (see Acts 2).

The oil of all oils began to flow because the King of all kings taught us the very principle: Close the Door—forgive—and the oil will flow.

Endnotes

1. Randall Worley, "Forgiveness is not an emotion, it's a decision"; http://www.emotionalcompetency.com/forgiveness.htm; accessed August 22, 2011.

2. Kin Hubbard (September 1868–December 1930), Chinese Proverb: "Nobody ever forgets where he buried the hatchet."

3. Abraham Lincoln, quoted in Andy Andrews, *The Young Traveler's Gift* (Nashville: Thomas Nelson, 2004).

4. Abraham Lincoln (February 1809–April, 1865); http://www.civilwarhome.com/endofwar.htm.

Chapter 5

DECIDED, NOT DIVIDED

This next principle really separates "the men from the boys," as they say.[1]

Consider it pure joy, my brothers and sisters, whenever you face trials of many kinds, because you know that the testing of your faith produces perseverance. Let perseverance finish its work so that you may be mature and complete, not lacking anything. If any of you lacks wisdom, you should ask God, who gives generously to all without finding fault, and it will be given to you. But when you ask, you must believe and not doubt, because the one who doubts is like a wave of the sea, blown and tossed by the wind. That person should not expect to receive anything from the Lord. Such a person is double-minded and unstable in all they do (James 1:2-8 NIV).

That's heavy duty. That's some big stuff right there. Let a person pray without doubting, without wavering, without being wishy-washy, without being undecided. The writer here declares that a person who can't make a decision or can't stick with a decision is dangerous to be around because that person is double-minded and unstable in everything that person does.

Even with the story of our little widow woman we find the necessity of this principle. It's not emphasized in the story, but nevertheless, it's part of this widow's transformation.

I mean, she had her sons knocking on every door. They were out digging in the bushes. They were getting empty pots from anywhere they could. They had *Big Gulp* cups and empty coffee cans—anything they could get their hands on. Their gathering ability was directly linked to the abundance they were going to receive down the road, so they were going all out.

But after *Taking Responsibility*, *Gathering the Ability*, and *Closing the Door* behind them, there had to be a decision made. Picture the scene: Here's this widow woman and her sons. They've worked hard up to this point, took some risks and lots of transition, and now they are all sitting and looking at each other in this house jammed full of empty pots.

Even though the neighbors were more than willing to give them empty pots, they're still wondering if they've lost their minds and how any of this makes any sense whatsoever because they are sitting in their little house looking at a plethora of empty pots and one little jar of oil. They were human just like us; they certainly must have had the thoughts that we sometimes deal with, *This is ridiculous! This is crazy! What are we doing? Am I just going to pour a drop of this oil into each pot or what?*

It was decision time! Even though the details were few and the mental capacity to perceive what lied ahead vague, the widow woman had to eventually look at her sons and say, "Let's do this!"

Many times God doesn't give you step-by-step instruction of what you're supposed to do next or how you're supposed to get it done. He just says, "Do it!" I've discovered over the years that the details don't usually come until I step out by faith and make a decision to do it!

When Jesus came walking on the water to His disciples, the apostle Peter said to Him, *"Lord, if that's really You, bid me to come"* (Matt. 14:28 KJV). Notice, Jesus didn't say, "Peter, pick your right foot up, lift it over the boat, gently set it down on the water, and just as you feel the moisture, run to…" No! He just said, "Come! Come on, Peter! You want to come, come!"

It was that way for the widow's family in Second Kings, it was that way for Peter, and it's still that way for us today. Most of the time you will just have to make a decision in your mind that you are going to run with what you have, stick with it, and see it through!

We have the benefit of reading this widow woman's story all at once so we know the end results. But they had no idea what was going to happen next. I can just picture it: she gets her little jar of oil and looks at her sons (by this time they're probably thinking, *Uhh, Mom! This is, well…maybe we should just go pack our bags now).*

At some point something had to happen, a decision point came when she said, "I'm going to do this! The prophet just said *pour*, so—I'm gonna pour. That's all the information I've been able to gather; that's all he's given me, but I have a word. I know the Lord is in this, and I'm gonna just pour." She made a decision in her heart, and the rest is history!

That's what I want to focus on in this chapter—the absolute necessity and power of a decided heart. I've seen so many people struggle with making a decision, especially a big decision. Indeed there should be some time for prayer, wisdom, and seeking counsel before making large decisions. However, I want to focus in on an even more particular part of this area of our lives—the ability to stick with a decision that we've already made.

Now this is a little challenging to fully unwrap because this can be easily mistaken as irresponsible. I suppose there will be times when we need to back away from a decision. Maybe there's been a divine change of direction. But what I see most of the time—more times than not—is people making a decision and then not sticking with it simply because the going gets rough and things get difficult.

Many will even play the religious card when things get challenging and say things like, "Well, I think the Lord is backing me out of this one." Wait a second! Please understand that just because things get terribly difficult along the way doesn't at all mean that you have made the wrong decision.

Many times adversity and struggle and trials and tribulations are proof that you are on the right path.

As a matter of fact, more times than not, it means you made the right decision. Many times adversities and difficulties only serve to prove that you are on the road to something greater than you have right now. As a pastor, I've seen this scenario unfold over and over again with people who have just recently made a decision to follow Christ. They come to the Lord, they hear about this Jesus and how He can change their lives, transform them—make everything new—all this—and He does. But then three months after they've been serving God with all their hearts, they're saying, "Pastor, my life has been a living hell since I came to the Lord. What is going on here? My family is fighting, everything is going crazy. I lost my job."

It's a clue. It's not the wrong decision, *believe me!* It's the right decision, and it just so happens that now those people have become a threat to the kingdom of darkness. The kingdom of darkness knows that its best chance with believers is to get them while they're new. Get them before the roots go down deep. Get them before they're battle strong.

And so the devil—what does he do? He can't steal that peace that Jesus gave them; he can't steal that joy, so he starts working in the circumstances around these believers, working in their environments, working in their families, working in their jobs. He starts pulling things away from them with the hopes of getting them to retreat, back off of this new road they're walking on (that ultimately leads to complete success—everlasting life) and get them to choose another path. It's important to realize that he doesn't care about their jobs or cars or houses. He doesn't want them personally...he wants the believers' faith!

Many times adversity and struggle and trials and tribulations are proof that you are on the right path. Other than in those rare exceptions, which I believe will exist even less after today, backing away from a decision, second-guessing yourself, and not giving 100 percent because you're actually still on the fence is a sure way to never prosper, never grow, never expand, and never succeed.

Over the years, I have witnessed this in ministries; I have witnessed this in marriages, in businesses, in people's personal goals and ambitions. As soon as things get turbulent, as soon as things get tough, many people start back-pedaling and looking for an exit strategy. Many times their vehicle of progress gets thrown into reverse. Suddenly that means the door to the past has to be reopened. Suddenly they're throwing everything they've gathered many times—including the voice of the Lord—out the window.

An undecided heart will cause you to look for an exit strategy when things get tough. Looking for an exit strategy usually leads you to open up doors to the past, forfeiting what was gathered (are you seeing the backward slide?), and before you know it, you're back to square one—blaming and accusing someone else or something else for why it didn't work.

It is extremely vital that you recognize right off the bat that the decisions that you enter into which have the ability to greatly alter your future are the very ones that will certainly be met with the most resistance. Usually, as soon as a door to the past closes, you are greeted by an opportunity to do something else which carries a need for a commitment—a decision.

The door is closed; now you have to make up your mind! However, the commitment of your heart—whether your heart is really in it all the way or not—is directly linked to whether you truly closed the door or not. Either you fully embrace each principle as you move forward, or they're certain to start breaking down as you go along the way.

When I think of an unwavering, committed, decided heart, I think of none other than Joshua. The truth of the matter is that Joshua inherited a nightmare. Think about this for a minute: Joshua had to take over the reins from Moses—probably the most recognized figure and name in the Bible next to Jesus. You could probably find somebody who doesn't know anything about the Bible and ask them if they can name one biblical figure, and they'd most likely say, "Moses."

We're talking about a huge historic figure here. We're talking about the man who personally received the Ten Commandments from God Almighty! We're talking about a man who was in the glory and the presence of the Lord so much that when he came down from the mountain, people had to shield their eyes to look at him. The Bible records that his face shined so brightly from being in the presence of the Lord that they had to put a cloth over his head just so the people could look at him!

We're talking about the man who lifted up his hand—put his rod out—and the Red Sea parted, a friend of God, a man of God. Yet even he could not seem to get these people he was leading to have a decided heart. How would you like to take over his position? As someone who has operated in leadership for many years now myself, I look at Joshua and say, "Good Lord! Joshua, you're the man!"

You don't get a decided heart after the promotion; it's the decided heart that gets you the job in the first place.

This was a huge challenge placed upon this young man's shoulders, but what stands out to me the most about Joshua was that he had a decided heart long before he was chosen to lead—which is one of the keys within this principle. You don't get a decided heart after the promotion; it's the decided heart that gets you the job in the first place.

Long before Joshua was a leader, way back under Moses—on Moses' team, on Moses' staff—he was a young man with a decided heart. I'm talking about a committed, *"Let's go do it, let's get after it, come on just give me the word and I'm gone"* type of commitment! This young man had such a decided heart that he was even willing to go against his peers.

Moses sent out 12 men to spy the land; ten came back with a negative report. Not Joshua and Caleb. They come back with a very different perspective. A decided heart will many times put you against the popular vote. It will put you against the majority. Not everybody's going to see your vision. Not everybody's going to want to go along with what your dream is. Yet Joshua was not swayed by what others said, because he had a decided heart.

Long before Joshua was the leader who took over for Moses, he was a young man being groomed by the very hand of God because of his ability to have a decided heart! While his peers came back with a bad report—all doom and gloom—Joshua and his sidekick, Caleb, came back with a report of faith, promise, and certain victory. His peers came back with reports of why it couldn't be done, "Did you see their armies?! Did you see how fortified their cities are! Did you see how big and powerful their warriors are?"

Now let me point out something here. These other ten leaders who Moses sent alongside Joshua and Caleb were not wimps and they weren't dummies. We might be tempted to picture these ten guys as weak chickens—"Oh, I don't think we can do it…I'm scared of fighting!" But no, no, no—these guys were warriors. They were battle-hardened soldiers who were leaders among their tribes. These guys were bad to the bone! It wasn't a matter of the biceps; it was a matter of the heart.

And Joshua—who was seeing the same challenges as the rest of them—still stood up and said, "Come on you guys! We can do this! We can take this land!" What separated Joshua and Caleb from the rest of these guys was a decided heart. They had reviewed the facts just like the ten. They had analyzed the situation at hand just like everybody else, but they also recognized that this was something that God had called them to do, and that changes everything. That's the game-changer right there, which is the same for the dreams and desires that are in your heart today.

Most of them—if they are good and noble—have been placed there by God Himself. With that in mind, Joshua displayed an attitude and a voice that said, "I'm going to do this, or I'm going to go down trying!" You know when someone has a decided heart because it is so matter-of-fact. "I'm going to do this, or I'm going to crash and burn trying." It was this unwavering commitment that began to move Joshua into his future position—long before Moses turned everything over to him—because he knew that he had a decided heart.

People will follow you everywhere. People will seek your wisdom and your advice all because you have a decided heart. Challenges that previously looked like mountains in your life will begin to melt at your feet when you have a decided heart.

Challenges that used to look like mountains will melt at your feet when you have a decided heart.

Even though it proved to be a fight most of the way for Joshua, even though it was a whole lot of trouble and a whole lot of turbulence, even though the trials were long and tribulations fierce—Joshua did the impossible by leading millions of people who needed a decided heart themselves into the Promised Land. Even years later, at the end of Joshua's life—now living in the Promised Land—he still lived by this principle. While others were still on the fence, Joshua is still saying, "You guys need to make a decision."

Joshua walks these people through the drill, goes back and starts to go through the list of past victories, "Here, I'll help you out—and I don't even care who you choose—just choose somebody." He says, "Look, if you want to serve these carved images from these other nations—gods of wood and stone— then do it. Or if you're going to serve the God who brought us through the Red Sea, who delivered us (and he goes through all the miracles), then do it. Just make a decision and stick with it. But just in case you're wondering about me, my decision is already made: *"As for me and my house, we will serve the Lord!"* (Joshua 24:15.)

Most people fail at what they attempt because of an undecided heart more than any other reason.

Have you ever been around people who make decisions with an undecided heart? They'll tell you about their decision that they're making, then they'll ask you about your opinion. They'll think about your opinion, and they'll go across town and ask their other friend about his opinion. Then they'll come back and ask you about the opinion of the other friend across town. Then they just take it to some random guy at Starbucks and see what he thinks.

They finally make a decision, and then they come back to you and ask you your opinion about their decision. Then they ask the other guy across town his opinion about their decision. Then they ask your opinion about his opinion of their decision—back and forth they go. They'll finally go one way or the other, and the problem is, it's an ongoing state of analysis. People like this spend so much time analyzing their decisions that they don't have any energy left to actually do what they decided to do.

Life is short! Get off the fence. Dive in and do something! Left, right, up, down—just go! The purpose of analysis is to come to a conclusion! It's not to continue analyzing. Make a move and stick with it. Here's the problem: the prospect of making a *right* decision scares people. But the truth of the matter is that nobody's going to make all the right decisions all the time. However, I believe that God has given us all the ability to make them right!

We may not make all the right decisions, but God has given us the ability to make the decision we make, *right*.

Think about that for a second. We may not make all the right decisions. But God has given us the ability to make the decision that we make, *right*. This might stretch you a little bit here, but stick with me.

Don't get caught up in the avalanche of endless opinion gathering. So many people finally make a decision, but then continue gathering opinions about the decision that they just made. My friend, this will kill your progress altogether! You will never move forward because you will always find somebody who thinks you're wrong. Always!

You may be thinking, *but how do I get past criticism—what other people think?* Here's a little exercise for you: Think about your favorite restaurant. Now go to your computer and run a search on that favorite restaurant (or even your favorite dish). I have a feeling that you will be able to quickly find people who think your favorite restaurant stinks! You will find people who think your favorite dish is terrible! Think about your favorite book, your favorite movie, your favorite person in the whole world.

Run another search. You'll find people ripping them up, people who hate them, people who think your favorite book is stupid—and on and on. If there are people who hate your favorite movie and favorite book and even your favorite people, then what makes you think you will get a free pass? I mean, you're going to have critics. Don't be stuck and don't be bound by everybody else's opinion. You will always find somebody who thinks your decision is wrong. However, an undecided or decided heart has a lot to do with how you make decisions and your conduct after the decision is made.

Yes, you should gather information. Yes, you should seek wisdom. Yes, you should seek counsel, which is why you need your personal Board of Directors. But after you've sought counsel and wisdom, you need to move forward with an attitude that says, "I'm going to do this or I'm going to die trying." That's a decided heart!

Let's go deeper with this. You will not always be able to know every little detail before you make a decision. As a matter of fact, most people can look back to five years ago and say, "Well, if I had known back then, what I know now, I probably would have done that a little differently." Here's the good news—at least you did something! The fact of the matter is, many others from five years ago who were there to capitalize on the same opportunity as you, did nothing because they couldn't get enough of the details to make their decision.

The opportunity is long gone now; it's over. But they're still getting opinions and doing research! Sometimes you're not always going to have every little detail to complete the picture. But you will have enough information to make a decision. In James 1:8 it says, *"a double-minded man, is unstable in all his ways."* All his ways! You know what *all* means in the Greek and the Hebrew, right? It means ***all!*** *"All his ways."* It touches everything. It touches the ministry you're in. It touches the marriage you're in. It touches the family you're in. It touches the business you're in. It touches your hopes, and it touches your dreams—you name it! It touches everything.

Have you ever talked to someone who was absolutely, positively 100 percent sure that God had led that person down a particular path until it got tough? Until all hell breaks loose—then, like magic, that person is 100 percent positively sure that God is leading them in the other direction. Somebody once said, "Hey, if you're going to live in 'wishy-washy land,' leave God out of it." He does not change His mind because times get tough. He does not change His mind because the going gets rough. Be very careful if you say, "God has led me here."

One of the best ways to keep a decided heart is to make sure the destiny is worth the hassle.

The apostle James, writing under the influence of the Holy Spirit, said that *people with an undecided heart are dangerous; unproductive; because they bring instability into everything they touch* (see James 1:7-8).

If you don't decide what's important in your life, if you don't decide what God truly called you to be a part of, you're going to end up spending your whole life changing paths, changing directions, and never going anywhere. One of the best ways to keep a decided heart—because it's challenging—is to make sure the destiny, the calling, the vision, or the goal of what you're working toward is worth the hassle. Is what you're believing for big enough to keep you? Is it worth the hassle? There's going to be a lot of hassle along the way. There's going to be a lot of problems.

Decided, Not Divided

Life can be a struggle. Success as a parent, success as a spouse, success as a business person, success as a leader, success in any area, at any level will be a struggle. It's going to be a struggle to maintain a decided heart. Otherwise what you're struggling for won't be worth the struggle in the first place. So you have to think big. You have to dream big. You have to believe big, or at least connect with somebody or a group that does so it can rub off on you.

**Is what you're believing
for, *big* enough to keep you?**

If what you're believing for and working toward is not big enough, you will be ambushed by bigger things every day that will eventually break you down. Somebody said it like this: "If you're hunting rabbits in tiger country, keep your eyes peeled for tigers. But if you're hunting tigers, just ignore the rabbits."

One of the characteristics of people with decided hearts is that they own their decisions. I like that! They don't blame, they don't say, "Well, uhh..." No, they own their decisions, and they have an attitude that politely says, "If you're with me, fine—I'm glad to have you along. If you're not, that's OK too, but I really don't care what you say or think about it." It's their decision. "If I fail, I own it. If I succeed, I own it."

Joshua said, "Hey, you guys need to make up your minds. Choose you this day whom you will serve. But your decision has zero effect on me. My heart's already decided. As for me and my house, we're going to serve the Lord" (see Josh. 24:15). In other words, "We are going to fulfill our destiny. If I have to take this land all by myself—I'm pressing on; I'm moving forward."

Not everybody who says they're going to be there till the end will be. But that should not sway you! That should not turn you! That should not change you! The people you thought were going to be on your side, but are not, might be a bigger group than you thought. Sometimes it's the people you really thought would be there who are the first to leave—and others whom you weren't too sure about will surprise you. You must not let that affect you. Do not let that cause you to waiver.

The critics are going to come out by the droves. The naysayers are going to line up all along the path that you have chosen and have their day in the sun, but you must press on.

If you worry all the time about what others think, you will end up having more confidence in their opinion than in yourself. And your future should not depend upon the permission and opinion of others. Again, this is where a personal Board of Directors comes in handy. Surround yourself with people who hear from God. Surround yourself with people who are successful. Outside of that, you just press on, and let the others say what they may. Believe me, they will. "I can't believe you're going to do that, at your age. I can't believe you're getting involved in that. I can't believe that you're going to try to start a business in this economy."

But sooner or later, you just have to take a stand and say, "There's a dream in my heart. I have to do this! It's now or never! I'm gonna go for it or die trying, but I will not sit around until everyone approves!"

Let me tell you a little bit about Christopher Columbus. Practically everybody in the whole world—at that time—thought Christopher Columbus was insane, *and they told him that too.* It took 19 years for Columbus to get financing for the voyages to go find new worlds. I think finally somebody financed him just to get rid of him. Seriously, the ridicule and criticism was awful because everybody in the world at that time believed the world was flat. They literally thought that they were financing a suicide mission. They believed that he was just going to sail right off the end of the earth into some great abyss. But Christopher Columbus believed the world was round. He believed that you could continue sailing on the surface of this round world and come all the way back around to where the journey started. He also believed that there were new lands to discover in the westward path.

I like what Christopher Columbus said, "Truth is truth. And if a million people believe something foolish it's still foolish."

He said, "Truth is never dependent upon the consensus of opinions." He continued in saying, "I have found that it is better to be alone acting on truth than to follow a gaggle of silly geese doomed to mediocrity."[2]

**A decided heart is a
heart that contains passion!**

Poor is the person whose future depends on the opinions of others. If you are afraid of criticism, you will die doing nothing. Criticism, condemnation, and complaints are creatures of the wind. They come and go on the breath of visionless people, but should have no power over you whatsoever.

A decided heart is a heart that contains passion! Passion is powerful. When you get passion about something—look out! I remember when I met that certain someone—*passion!* I know my heart was decided because I got really passionate about it. Full pursuit—time was irrelevant. Sleep was irrelevant. Food was irrelevant. *Where is she?*

A decided heart will contain passion, and passion will help you overcome insurmountable obstacles. Suddenly, your life will become a statement. Suddenly your life will become an example to others. Others will see their future in your eyes. Passion inspires others to join in on your pursuit. Passion breeds conviction and turns mediocrity into excellence.

Thus, the most amazing display of courage, redemption, and destiny ever displayed is referred to as the Passion of the Christ. I'm glad He had a decided heart. It was a decided heart that took Him past the whipping post. It was a decided heart that took Him past the spit in His face and ripping out of His beard. It was a decided heart that caused Him to remain nailed to a cross—when He could have called angels down and wiped out everyone. It wasn't the nails that held Him on the cross; it was a decided heart.

An undecided heart cannot contain passion; it will withhold success in any area. Your greatest victories and accomplishments will require the emotional balance of a decided heart. For when you are confronted with challenges—and many will come—a decided heart will search for solutions. An undecided heart will search for an escape.

**An undecided heart
cannot contain passion; it will
withhold success in any area.**

A decided heart never waits for conditions to be exactly right. You want to know why? Because they're never exactly right! I believe that is why God gave every person a measure of faith. Just take that first step. Just do it.

Indecision limits God in His ability to perform miracles in your life. *Indecision ties the hands of God.* The reason many people aren't seeing the miracles they want to see is because they haven't chosen a path and stuck with it long enough. A decided heart causes you to stick with it, and sticking with it long enough ultimately unties the hands of God to release just exactly what you need in your life.

I believe that many times God gets ready to act on someone's behalf, but before He does, the individual once again backs out and takes another path. I wonder how many times people are on the verge of a miracle or an open door or divine contact, yet they waiver, back away, and start over again somewhere else, once again totally missing it? Sticking with something will give God the opportunity to work miracles in your life.

I believe God is the giver of the dreams and visions that we have in our hearts—if they're good and noble—and to wait and wonder, to doubt and to be indecisive, is to disobey God. We never think about it like that, but it is so. Romans 4 talks about Abraham and says that even though he didn't know where he was going, even though he didn't know when he would get there or how God would perform this promise, he pressed on! The Bible says, *"he did not waiver at the promise of God through* [doubt or] *unbelief but, was strengthened in faith, giving glory to God"* (Rom. 4:20).

Contrary to hope,
hope believed anyway.

Contrary to hope, hope believed anyway. Contrary to what he saw in the natural, he believed anyway. Even though the "right now" didn't look anything like what was supposed to be, he continued to believe. How? He had a decided heart! Even though Abraham did not always make the right decisions, he made each decision right by continuing to press forward as God had commanded. *"Let us hold fast the confession of our hope without wavering, for He who promised is faithful"* (Heb. 10:23).

Don't look at an exit strategy when things get tough, when disagreements come, and when trouble arises; otherwise you will inevitably become a person who time and time again *almost* succeeded, *almost* made a difference, *almost* made an impact, *almost* broke through, *and almost* had a testimony. You can't get to a testimony without a test.

In this *Principle of a Decided Heart*, I am once again reminded of a story I read about Hernando Cortez—a *conqueror* by trade. That's not politically correct today, but back in 1519—there were bankers, doctors, farmers, and conquerors. Hernando Cortez was a conqueror—that's what he did. It's a true story about a vast treasure that many armies—conquerors—had tried to take for 600 years.

**You can't get to a
testimony without a test.**

It had remained in the hands of a highly fortified island people for centuries. Many had tried to overpower these people and take the treasure of gold, jewels, silver—a real pirates' treasure—but none had succeeded. Over the centuries, it became the most sought-after collection ever.

Army after army would go and invade this place where the treasure was, only to be defeated time and time again. For 600 years these people had successfully held off armies and pirates and had kept this treasure within their control, but along came Cortez.

Cortez studied carefully others who had been defeated and other miserable attempts to obtain this treasure. Finally he made a decision that he too would set out on this quest. He took a different approach from the others who had gone before and immediately started interviewing the prospective men who would head out with him on this endeavor. He began to ask each one what they would do with their share of the loot. He asked them to imagine how their lives would change and how their family's lives would change. He asked them, "How will you spend the money?"

You see what he was doing—he was starting to build a vision within them. "Think about it," he would say. "Don't think about now—think about afterward—how is it going to change your life?" Cortez started interviewing these men and getting them thinking and getting them dreaming, and he ended up with 600 soldiers and 100 sailors committed to the cause.

In 11 ships they went out to conquer this area and take this treasure. But even on this long journey in the rough seas, some of those who were not so committed in the beginning started going, "Cortez, is it really that important? My life's not that bad, really." People started questioning and complaining, but Cortez held strong and said, "No, no, no men. We're going for it. We are going forward!"

Some of those, whom he thought would be the strongest, became the biggest whiners. But he kept saying, "We're going forward." After experiencing this for weeks and weeks on the turbulent seas, they finally landed on the Yucatan Peninsula. As they all gathered waiting for orders, thinking Cortez was about to say, "OK, you guys go left and we're going to go right, and if the shooting starts happening, we'll meet over here," but instead, he gave a very different order. He said, "Burn the boats!"

His general's chin hit the ground. The bewildered general said, "But, but, but, but…excuse me, sir!"

"You heard me," said Cortez, "burn the boats!" As everyone looked at him as if he had lost his mind, Cortez spoke up loudly so that everyone was sure to hear him clearly. He said, "Men, if we leave this island, we're going to be leaving on their boats! Burn the boats!"

Guess what happened? Those men took that treasure that day. You want to know why? Because their choices were take it or die.[3]

I have a few questions for you: What boats of excuses and limited beliefs are still floating in your mind? What boats of "what was" are keeping you from getting "what can still be"? What boats need to be burned in your life today?

My greatest desire in writing this book is to help people become decided, not divided! Families, churches, businesses, teams, countries—decided, not divided! If we would begin to burn all the exit strategies, all the Plan B's, we too could conquer any obstacle and any foe!

James 4:8 says, *"…Purify your hearts, you double-minded."* Think about those few words. *"Purify your hearts, you double-minded."* Double-mindedness—indecision—is a heart condition, and an undecided heart can never please God.

This is where we need to get really serious about this principle because we just read that a double-minded person is unstable in *all* ways; it touches everything. That means it comes right into our homes, right into our relationships, right into our Christianity or salvation. In other words, "I believe in God, but because I have an undecided heart, I struggle with trusting Him."

A double-minded person is unstable in *all* ways; it touches everything!

Do you want to succeed as a Christian? Do you want an intimate relationship with God? Do you want, like Moses, to be called *a friend of God*? Do you want to be visited by the Almighty? Get a decided heart and—like Abraham—start trusting God against all odds. Decide to do everything you can do each day. And even when that's not enough, still out of your mouth must come these words, "God can, God will, and I still believe that it's going to happen. He is able, He is willing, He is working on it right now. It's going to happen because out of the abundance of my heart, my mouth speaks!" (See Luke 6:45.)

You have a vision in your heart today for a reason. Those dreams that are in your heart for you, your family, and your future are there for a reason. To wait and wonder, to doubt and be indecisive, would be to deny the Word of God over your life altogether and to forfeit what is still possible. Have a decided heart, embrace your destiny, and be everything God created you to be.

Endnotes

1. "Separate the men from the boys," *Cambridge Dictionary of American Idioms* (Cambridge: Cambridge University Press, 2006).

2. Source unknown; attributed to Christopher Columbus.

3. *"Burn the boats! The Story of Cortez,"* in Anthony Pagden, trans. *Letters from Mexico* (New Haven, CT: Yale University Press, 2001).

Chapter 6

JUST DO IT

History remembers the bold! Everyone who stands out to you and me throughout history does so because they were in some way people of action!

As with our widow woman, it wasn't the tremendous instructions that she received that changed her life; it was her actions. Someone can give you the greatest investment tip in the world, and someone can tell you that they're giving away free cars down the street to everyone who shows up before noon. You can hear and receive tremendous instructions and fascinating secrets, but they are completely powerless until acted upon!

Elisha, (one of the most amazing prophets that ever lived) gave our little widow woman four verses of life-changing instructions (see 2 Kings 4:1-4). They were detailed, precise, and loaded with potential, but they would have become as powerless as the words of a fairy tale if she never acted upon them.

The first two words of verse 5 in Second Kings 4:5 says, *"She went...."* Those two words might seem like just everyday, normal-average, ordinary words to some people, but I see a whole story in them. When I read *she went*, I see action. I see the activation of the miraculous.

I see a desperate woman with a made-up mind and a decided heart springing into action even though the process seemed absurd. She went. She got up off of the couch of discouragement, turned off the television of *unproductivity*, got out of the living room of depression, stepped out of the house of despair, and said, "Hello endless possibilities! I'm coming after you with full force!"

I see a woman who suddenly turned the whole world into her classroom! I see a woman who recognized that it's not enough to hear about it, but rather it's "Doing it" that makes all the difference in the world! She went, she gathered, she closed the door, she poured, and the oil flowed (or you could say, "the miracle" happened).

In the words *she went*, I see a lady determined to reposition herself for a breakthrough! I see her making a purposeful effort to intersect with an opportunity. I don't know if I can express to you in words the absolute necessity of doing whatever it takes to reposition yourself to receive, but I'll try.

So many times people get stuck in a rut. So many times people get comfortable in the familiar and miss their moment! I have found that repositioning yourself is one of the keys within

this *God Principle of Taking Action*, which unlocks unbelievable potential. Now please understand, repositioning yourself
doesn't mean changing jobs every other month or moving to a
different location every couple of years.

No, rather I'm simply talking about being flexible, adapt-
ing, not letting yourself come under the false persuasion that's
there only one way to do something. Persistence is another key
to being blessed, but persistence doesn't necessarily mean doing
the same thing over and over until it works! Persistence means
never giving up, even if you have to try five different methods
until it finally works.

Many people find themselves very frustrated because they
have been persistent in their endeavor, yet it still hasn't worked.
Even though I encourage you to *never give up, I would sug-
gest that* you should continue to be persistent by trying a new
method. Reposition yourself and come at it again from a different angle, come at it with a new perspective and see what
happens then.

Have you ever ignored the instructions that came in the
box of your child's new swing set? (I'm probably, mainly speaking to my fellow brothers here.) *It looks simple enough; how difficult can it be, right?* So you worked and worked and worked
on that one little section—you know, that section that had that
weird little piece that looked like it was developed on Mars.
And after persistently trying it 14 different ways, you finally
dig the instructions out of the bottom of the box that you
already threw away to see what in the world you were supposed

to do to make it fit? After looking at those instructions for a few minutes, it hits you—you have that "ah ha" moment, and suddenly everything makes sense and falls into place. It wasn't that you weren't persistent; it's just that you needed a bit of revelation, a new perspective, and suddenly progress is once again happening.

That's what this book is all about really. I'm hoping to show you some really important stuff in *the* life manual itself, the Bible, with the hopes that you will have some "ah ha" moments and reposition yourself (or the way you've been trying to make it work) so you can once again make progress. To me, that's how I define success—*progress*.

All of that leads me to my next point about being a person of action. Sometimes it is not that you're *not* doing anything, but rather that you need to do something *differently*.

Sometimes it is not that you're not doing anything, but rather you need to do something *differently*.

Notice again our little widow woman. Elisha gave her some pretty strange and unusual instructions. As I mentioned earlier, she understood borrowing (which had put her in this awful situation to start with), but borrowing empty pots? It kind of sounded like the old prophet had been out in the sun too long. That didn't seem to make much sense at all. However, Elisha had specifically given her instructions that were out of *the norm* because this woman needed some extraordinary results!

Many times just doing *the norm* won't get the job done. And many times we really can't break out of our routine unless we purposely do something different. I say, *purposely*, because we very seldom will do it automatically! As a matter of fact, many times we have to be pushed out of our normality kicking and screaming, but after experiencing better results, we later look back and ask ourselves, "What took me so long to change?"

Purposely try to meet new people; purposely jog a different path tomorrow. Purposely say "hi" to that elderly man down the street who you see sitting in his garage every day. Who knows what kind of a life he has had? Maybe he's a war veteran; maybe he owned a hardware store for many years. Maybe he won a medal in the 1948 summer Olympics? Who knows what he might say to you that makes you tilt your head a little sideways and wonder. Who knows what seed he may plant in your mind, what perspective you might walk away with.

Just do something different; try a different angle, and take a new approach. Reposition yourself for a breakthrough! Elisha suggested to this widow woman that she do something that she had most certainly never done before, knowing that she needed results that she most certainly had never seen before! If you want to end up in different intersections, then you need to take a different path. This woman needed to intersect with an amazing opportunity. She needed some serious results, so she took action, regardless of the unfamiliarity of the method.

Most of us have already figured out a long time ago that very few (if any) opportunities come knocking on our front doors while we sit there watching television. I purposely say "most" of us because there are still those who really need some knowledge in these areas.

Actually, many people are frustrated with their lives, frustrated that things aren't happening for them like they'd like, frustrated because the opportunities seem few. However, when you sit down and talk with them about what they're actually doing to increase the probability of opportunities, they kind of look at you like a deer caught in the headlights. *You mean I'm actually supposed to be doing something to create opportunities? I thought I was just supposed to be ready to act when the opportunity arose?* This is a bit of a problem. Many tell themselves, "As soon as an opportunity arises, I'm going to grab it with both hands. I'm going to go after it with all I have!" And of course they should, if a great opportunity appears, but what if the opportunity never shows up? Better yet, what if the opportunity is waiting on them? Suddenly they have a stalemate. They are waiting on the opportunity, the opportunity is waiting on them, and they spend another month, another year, with zero breakthroughs.

**People who are blessed,
are *blessed*, not *lucky*.**

It's imperative that we understand that people who are blessed are *blessed*, not *lucky!* The people we look up to, the people we admire (successful people) are probably not *who* they are or *where* they are because someone pulled up to their house one day in a dump truck named opportunities and then dumped everything that they would ever need on their front door step. No, blessed people are not lucky; rather, blessed people are people of action; they are "doers" of the work (and if they're really smart, doers of the Word, too). (See James 1:22-25.)

Actions create opportunity! Over and over when you look at the promises and blessings in the Bible, you will always find a prerequisite. Time and time again we find God saying, "If you'll do this, then I'll do that. If you'll live according to this, then this is what you can expect to receive." (See Genesis 4:7, 6:13,18, 20:7, 22:17; Exodus 23:7, 23:22; Deuteronomy 7:12-16, 8 and 11.)

Looking at the Book of James once again, we see the great apostle, who spoke about the necessity of being decided, the danger of being double-minded and the liberation of having a decided heart. He also talked about the importance of being a "doer"—a person of action.

Do not merely listen to the word, and so deceive your-selves. Do what it says. Anyone who listens to the word but does not do what it says is like someone who looks at his face in a mirror and, after looking at himself, goes away and immediately forgets what he looks like. But the who-ever looks intently into the perfect law that gives freedom, and continues in it—not forgetting what they have heard, but doing it—they will be blessed in what they do (James 1:22-25 NIV).

The blessing you desire requires action! And the apostle James makes it perfectly clear that if you only "hear it" (without consistently doing it), you are completely deceived if you actually think that something is going to change because of it. It doesn't matter how tremendous the sermon was, how inspiring the motivational speech was, or how enlightening the instructions were (even if those instructions are from the Bible); they will all die within you quickly if they are not activated in the doing process!

**The blessing you
desire requires action!**

There is a direct connection made in these verses between "doing" and being blessed. I love people of action! I love hanging around people who know how to get things done. I'm not so inspired by those who *talk* about what they're going to do, but I love people of action!

When I think of a person of action, I quickly think of David (the shepherd boy and eventual king of Israel). David was a do-it man; he was a man of action all the way. When others around seemed to complain and come up with all the reasons why it couldn't be done, David already had a plan of action, and he was "chomping at the bit" to get started.

One day when the armies of Israel were lined up in battle array against the Philistine armies, David got his chance to act. David had been sent by his father to take some provisions to his older brothers who were soldiers under King Saul. When David reached the battlefield, he was appalled at the insults he heard being hurled across the field by the Philistine's champion Goliath. This actual giant of a man was mocking and taunting David's brothers and all the nation of Israel. David instantly sprang into action and shouted out; "Somebody's got to do something!"

However, David was quickly rebuked by his older brothers (who were seasoned warriors) and they told him to run along—go back to tending sheep (in other words, you're not man enough to even be in the army, let alone fight this giant Goliath). That didn't go over to well though, because you can't just tell a man of action like David to "run along"…even if he was just a young man still wet behind the ears.

No way! Men of action don't open their mouths unless they're prepared to do something about it, and *Prepared* was David's middle name!

Before you know it, this young man made his way to the leader of the army (King Saul himself) and is telling him that he can get the job done—and that's exactly what he did!

While everybody else was coming up with every reason under the sun why the mission was impossible, David had the audacity to tell King Saul, "Not only will I take him out...but I'll DO IT without any armor...and I'll DO IT with only a sling and a stone!" And he did!

A DO IT man or woman will always figure out a way to get it done, even if everybody laughs and thinks they're crazy. But when the giant hit the ground, the laughing ceased, and David went from nobody to somebody in 60 seconds—all because he was a man of action!

David was a do-it man; he knew how to get it done. While it seemed that all of the others found excuses, David found the tenacity to press forward and get the job done. Good things come to those who act!

I heard a story once about a young man who visited a very wealthy and successful man's home. The older, seasoned gentleman took the younger fellow on a little tour of his estate. The young man walked around with his mouth wide open admiring the fine furnishings, expensive art, and luxurious surroundings. After taking it all in for a bit, the young man turn to his accommodating host and said, "You are so lucky!" Without missing a beat, the wealthy man chuckled a bit and replied, "Yeah, it's funny though…'cause it seems the harder I work, the luckier I get."

Blessings do not come to those who wait; blessings come to those who act! Most of the time when the Scriptures say to "be still" or to "wait on God," it is referring to one of two things: 1) being still on the inside—having a calm assurance on the inside, trusting God on the inside while still working hard on the outside—or 2) having a time of rest with the purpose of renewing your strength so you can once again run and take action! (See Deuteronomy 4:5; 1 Samuel 2:3; 1 Kings 8:39; Proverbs 13:16; Ecclesiastes 5:3; Luke 17:14; Acts 8:36; Psalm 46:10, 25:3, 25:21, 27:14, 37:7-9; Isaiah 30:18, 40:31; Acts 22:16.)

Blessings do not come to those who wait; blessings come to those who act!

Many times Christians will see God as *Provider* (which indeed He most certainly is), but make the mistake of thinking that all they have to do is just sit back and wait because eventually He'll come through. As a pastor, I often hear people say, "Well, I'm just waiting on God…." Can I let you in on a little secret? Most of the time, God is waiting on us!

The problem with that mentality is that it contradicts specific divine laws and *God Principles* threaded all throughout the Scriptures. One might argue that "God said He would supply my every need" (see Phil. 4:19). To that I would have to reply, "He also said that He feeds the birds, but I've never seen Him throw a worm in their nest!" (See Luke 12:24). God created the worm; He placed the worm in the general vicinity of the nest, but the bird still has to get out of the nest, fly around a while, spot that little worm, and then dive down and get it!

Imagine if our little widow woman never "went." Even though the instruction she received held the keys to an incredible miracle, they would have fallen to the ground powerless if she had never taken action! The apostle James directly links the blessed life to action. *Those who are doers of the work, these ones will be blessed in whatever they do* (see James 1:25). God blesses what you do, not what you hear. As a person of action, you are going to have to learn how to stomp fear underneath your feet and say *"yes!"*

Don't let intimidation or insecurity cause you to say "no" and miss your moment! Rise up, push back against fear and timidity, look at yourself in the mirror, and say, "I am a do-it person! I can do this!"

**Most of the time,
God is *waiting* on us!**

I remember coming up through the ranks in both business and as a pastor. In business, I can remember having the opportunity to purchase larger facilities for our manufacturing plant as we continued to grow and expand. I can also remember being approached with the opportunity to contract on projects that were far bigger than our ability at the time. Of course fear always jumps right in the middle of everything and tries to point out all the things that could go wrong, all the mishaps that could occur, and the disasters of biting off more than you can chew.

Many times I had to fight back the lies of fear, and even though I didn't have it all figured out at the time, I opened my mouth and said, "Yes, we can handle your project no problem. Yes, we'll buy that building and move our factory!"

Now I will admit that many times I walked away with an immense battle going on in my head. The battle sounded something like this, ***What are you thinking? It's OK. It's OK. We can do this… What? Are you crazy? Have you lost your ever-lovin' mind!?*** *Chill out, man! We got this! We'll hire more guys, buy more equipment. We'll figure it out…we **can do this!***

Of course, I realize that there are limitations, but you can accomplish a lot more than fear wants you to believe. Fear is nothing more than a misuse of the God-given creativity you and I have in our brains. That same creativity that you can use to dream and imagine great things is the same creativity that fear tries to arrest and cause you to imagine all the bad that could happen. Put fear under your feet and learn to say *"Yes!"*

These same opportunities to run away or to say "yes" happened in my pastoral or public speaking development as well. When I was only about 20 years old, I walked into the front door of the church I attended one Sunday morning to find my pastor standing there in the foyer waiting on me. With an unusual look on his face—kind of a little smirk, now that I think back about it—he walked up to me, looked me right in the eyes, and said, "Son, I'd like you to be the speaker for today's service. Can you do that for me?"

Now it's of the utmost importance that I explain to you that I wasn't a junior pastor at the time. I wasn't anything! As a matter of fact, I hadn't spoken publicly more than maybe a time or two, if that. Furthermore, he was giving me about a 30-minute advance warning! It's not like he was saying, *Son, could you put something together and share with us in a few weeks?* Which would have still been a huge challenge in itself. But no, no, no—he was asking me to do it in 30 minutes without any prior warning!

Of course, any normal human being would have come up with some kind of great excuse (like one of the million going through my head at the time) or would have run far away and never come back—yet out of my mouth came, "Yes sir."

As beads of sweat instantly formed on my head, my pastor smiled really big, shook my hand vigorously, and said, "Great! I'll introduce you when it's time to come up," and with that he walked away.

Have you ever prayed with all your heart that you would wake up—hoping that you were dreaming—while knowing full well that you weren't? Looking back, it's quite possible that at that very moment I begged God to take me straight to Heaven at the ripe old age of 20!

I remember a horrific mental battle instantly raging. *What are you thinking? Do you know what you just said "yes" too? What will you speak about? You have absolutely nothing prepared. As a matter of fact, you don't even know how to prepare! Hurry, chase him down…tell him you're feeling sick, tell him you forgot your Bible, tell him anything, but "yes"!*

It's been 20 years since that *yes* happened, and I now pastor a wonderful church and speak regularly to crowds of 10,000-15,000 people. You see, I learned early on that it's not always the *best* who are blessed, but the *yes* who are blessed!

It's not always the *best* who are blessed, but the *yes* who are blessed!

It wasn't about how good my sermon was on that day (and let me tell you, it was baa-ad…really bad…and *very* short), but rather it was about being obedient to my leadership, who I ultimately knew wanted the best for me. It was about learning to stomp fear under my feet and say "yes." I believe that it was a simple *"Yes"* like that that spring-boarded me toward future opportunities! "Yes" at the right time will continue to draw opportunities toward you. While "no" at the wrong time will cause opportunities to avoid you like the plague.

Please understand me. I'm not saying that you should say "yes" to every person around you all of the time. Of course there's a time to say "no"—that's a whole other subject, perhaps a whole other book—but there's also a time to say "yes." This is especially true when you're being asked to step up and do something with any kind of nobility or sincerity.

You must stomp fear under your feet and say "yes"! Will it be challenging? Of course it will! However, it will also come with great rewards if you persistently press ahead. Take back your ability to move, grow, and succeed. Stomp fear under your feet where it belongs! May all fear be exposed as the powerless vapor imposter that it is in the name of Jesus!

Fear has no authority over those who know who they are! Never again need you fear opinion; never again need you fear gossip or the shallow words of the comfortable. Never again need you fear failure. For I submit to you today that failure is a myth! It only exists in the minds of those who give up, and you do not give up, because you are a person of action, one of a do-it generation—the giant-killing, mountain-moving children of the Most High God!

You can do this! You must do this! For the alternate is unacceptable. Act now or the years will slip by quicker and quicker, and before you know it, you'll be saying, "I wish I would have at least given it a try." I would rather see people step out, give it their best shot, and then fall flat on their face, than to see them fail automatically by doing nothing!

Calvin Coolidge said, "We can't do everything at once, but by God we can do something at once!"[1]

As a pastor I have approached many people over the years (never as my former pastor approached me of course) asking them if they could step up and serve in one area or the other. And I have had every kind of response you can imagine, "Uhhh—I don't think I'm ready for that," or "Who me? Sorry the timing is not good." This is the one that I hear the most, "Uhhh…let me pray about that, and I'll get back to you." That one always makes me chuckle a bit because I know it really doesn't have anything to do with prayer or getting God's permission!

Can I just give you a tip here: you're not always going to feel ready or qualified or worthy, but—here's the tip—that's probably one of the reasons you were chosen in the first place. Most leaders aren't looking for Mr. Big Head or Mrs. Incredibly Qualified; they're just looking for those who have a good attitude, have displayed some leadership qualities, and are willing to give it their best! Feel free to let them know that you don't feel qualified or worthy, but then also let them quickly know that you're honored and that you'll give it your 100 percent.

"I'll pray about it..." Can you imagine Joshua saying that to Moses?

Moses: "Joshua, I'm gathering some of the finest leaders I have to go and survey the land that God Almighty has given us. I need you to be one of those guys Joshua, this is very important. I can count on you, right?"

Joshua: "Oh wow...uh, yeah...about that...I've been meaning to actually talk to you about something. Uh, the wife and I just signed up for a knitting class on Wednesday nights. Actually, I've been meaning to let you know that we won't be able to make it to the leader's meetings for the next six months or so and, uh, as far as this special mission...uh, yeah. That's gonna be tough. Let me pray about it, Moses, and I'll get back to you."

So many times people place things that don't really matter that much over other things or opportunities that do, and then ten years down the road they wonder why everyone else seems to be getting all the breaks instead of them. Be a person of action! Take hold of opportunities to learn, grow, serve, and make a difference because too many no's or wishy-washy responses will cause opportunities to start avoiding you, leaving you wondering down the road, *What's wrong with me? Why do I seem invisible? Where'd all the opportunities go?*

Learn to say "yes," even if that "yes" is to yourself! Get up tomorrow morning, look at yourself in the mirror, and say *"Yes!"*

"Yes, I'm going to get out there and shake the bushes today!" "Yes, I'm going to make some new contacts today!" "Yes, I'm going to say hi to that elderly man down the street and strike up a conversation with him." "Yes, I'm going to the gym today!" "Yes, I'm going to jog a new path today." "Yes, I'm going to make that call, accept that position to serve, do something out of the ordinary today." "Yes, I'm going to do something that scares me half to death to think about it. I have to. I'm a person of action!"

Most of the time, opportunities follow action, not vice versa. Be a person of action, make the first move, get out there, and go for it. It's important to recognize that the encouragement you need, the opportunities you're looking for, the knowledge and information that will change your situation will usually come through other people. And guess what? Those people are "out there." They're most likely not going to come looking for you and rescue you off your couch of despair.

Most of the time, opportunities follow action, not vice versa.

Let's look at this from a spiritual perspective for a moment. Why do you think it is that when the enemy of our soul (the devil) sends the spirits of depression and discouragement, people automatically start withdrawing, pulling away from others, and regrettably vegging out all day on the couch watching television? It's simple; the devil knows that your breakthrough, your freedom, your miracles come through you acting upon *God Principles!*

He knows that people of action are dangerous to the kingdom of darkness because such people will eventually figure out a way through the storm, a way over the mountain. Furthermore, these people will eventually enjoy amazing marriages, great friends, and wise investments. In other words, they'll be blessed in every area of their lives and in all that they do. These people become a threat to the enemy because they literally bring glory to God in every aspect of their lives, which exposes and shatters every lie and plan of darkness!

Since the devil knows this full well, he sends his separator spirits of depression and discouragement in an attempt to stop you from becoming everything that God has already called you to be. Don't let these spirits control you; don't let them pull you backward. Don't let them pull you away from opportunities that lie ahead. Don't let insecurity cause you to say *"no"*—making you miss your moment over and over again! No way! Be a person of action, be a do-it person! Square up your shoulders, stick your chest out, take a deep breath, put your "I-got-this" face on, and *go after it!*

The shepherd boy, David, wasn't qualified to be a giant killer; he just did it! The 12 men Jesus chose to be the original apostles of the church were not qualified in any certain terms. Jesus just walked by them one day and saw them all doing something, so He said, "Hey, I have an even higher assignment for you; follow Me."

Many times your next opportunity will arise because you're doing something. When someone approaches you about stepping up, helping in a certain area at church, on the job, in the community, it's probably because you've already been doing something which sends out messages to everyone around you that says, "This is a person of action who can get it done!" Many times you'll be asked to do something that isn't even remotely related to your experience. But that's irrelevant! A doer is a doer is a doer is a doer! And a person of action will figure out a way to get it done! People are always watching you to try to figure out who you are. Seize the moment, take hold of each opportunity, and be a person of action. You can do it!

Endnote

1. Andy Andrews, "6 Keys to Becoming a Person of Action," *The Complete Business Resource*: BABM Feb. 2009. <http://www.babm.com/values/6-Keys-to-Becoming-a-Person-of-Action.htm>; accessed Sept. 27, 2011. Calvin Coolidge.

Chapter 7

I AM CONTENT

I find it interesting that the very first thing that God Himself commanded Adam and Eve to do was *"Be fruitful and multiply, fill the earth, subdue it; have dominion over* [it]…" (Gen. 1:28).

Think about that for a minute. God had just created everything that Adam and Eve needed to sustain themselves. They were in paradise—you could say, "They had it made." Yet God immediately reveals something in the first chapter of Genesis that should help clarify the true meaning of *contentment*.

Many have used the word *contentment* as a crutch to justify their complacency. Many have grown up with a misunderstanding of this word that has been passed down from generation to generation—causing good people to settle for less than what God has for them.

I've heard misguided people scold those around them who endeavor to grow, expand, and prosper at new levels of success. They will say things to them like, "You already have more than most people. Why don't you learn to be content?" The implication, of course, is that if you desire more than what you have now or more than what the *average* person has, you're just greedy! In fact, this is not true at all!

Certainly greed is prevalent in our society. And greed is ugly and awful! But we need to have an awakening to the *God Principles* of growth, prosperity, and abundance and then clearly separate them from the perverted evil versions, which certainly include greed! God gave Adam and Eve strict orders to "multiply." Many people think that just means having children, but nothing could be further from the truth. When God said, "be fruitful," He was indeed talking about having children and having the seed within to reproduce. However, *multiply* means something totally different. The definition of *multiply* is this: "to increase in whatever respect; to bring in abundance; to enlarge; to excel exceedingly; to heap on or pile-up" (Strong's Concordance).

Is that amazing or what? God was specifically telling Adam and Eve—who technically already had everything that they needed—"I want you to expand, excel, and increase abundantly. That's My will and plan for your life!" What? This is very different from the mentality that says, "You have enough; you should just learn to be content!"

Have you ever been around people with that mentality? A lot of people (especially within Christianity) grow up with this idea that you really shouldn't ask God for *more* than you need. They make statements like, "Well, all your needs are met—so you just need to be content." Wait just a minute! How does that collate with God Himself instructing us to *multiply*? Houston, we have a problem.

Let me give you some revelation that will help you really embrace contentment and prosperity at the same time. Contentment shouldn't be a state of mind that you slip into when all your needs are met. In actuality, you should be content even if all your needs are *not* met! Why is that? Contentment is an attitude, not an ambition!

Contentment is an attitude, not an ambition! It is an attitude of gratitude!

Contentment is an attitude of gratitude, and when God calls on us to be *content*, He is reminding us to be thankful for and appreciative of what we have now.

Let me talk to you about the *Grateful Heart Principle*. This simple, but not-so-small principle is literally the key to prospering at new levels. When you remember to be thankful and you purposely embrace gratitude, things will begin to happen for you and in you that will absolutely cause you to be more successful than ever. A lot of prospering and truly being blessed has to do with attitude, demeanor, and mindset. With that said, it's vital to understand that you can't be grateful and hateful at the same time! You can't be grateful and spiteful at the same time. Gratitude is your spiritual penicillin, which will crush the spiritual infection of discouragement and will eliminate all emotional infections in your life!

So many times we look high and low for the secret for success or the key to really enjoying life, and all the while it's right there in front of us—so simple but not always so easy—gratitude, thankfulness, true contentment for what we already have!

Gratitude causes you to operate in the correct mindset. This in return draws the right people toward you, as well as the right opportunities and connections. It also causes you to work smarter and with more focus because a grateful person appreciates having the opportunity to pursue dreams and is thankful for the progress already made!

A grateful person appreciates having the opportunity to pursue dreams.

As you truly begin to master this principle, you will find yourself becoming grateful for things that drive most people crazy. For example, I can get all bent out of shape about that flat tire that came at the wrong time and the wrong place. I can let those negative emotions snowball until I say things I shouldn't have and act hatefully toward my wife—who had nothing to do with it—eight hours later when I get home. *Or* I can look at that flat tire as a reason to be thankful, because it is proof that I have a car. The guy walking to work or the lady taking public transportation to the grocery store might very well look at your flat tire as the smallest of inconveniences to have such a privilege as their very own car! That broken window on your house—is it a source of contention or a reason to be thankful? Remember, that broken window on your house is yet again proof that you're not homeless!

Now as great as that all is, gratitude creates an even more important factor than everything just mentioned. Gratitude will draw your heavenly Father toward you and cause a divine connection to occur. Just as we parents—in the natural—desire our children to be thankful and grateful toward us by displaying a sincere attitude of appreciation, so our heavenly Father desires the same.

The psalmist David gives us a sneak peak of just how powerful gratitude is. This is the same David whom God Himself called, *"A man after My own heart"* (Acts 13:22). David wrote, *"Enter into His gates with thanksgiving…"* (Ps. 100:4). In other words, gratitude is the key that opens the King's gate. I don't have to hope it happens, and I don't have to try to make it happen. The gates to the courts of the King of Heaven open automatically when gratitude is my attitude and thankfulness is my language!

The gates to the courts of the King of Heaven open automatically when gratitude is my attitude and thankfulness is my language!

It's so simple, but not always so easy to do. Why is that? The fact of the matter is that there is a negative side to life! There is right and wrong, good and evil, which means that there is a constant war for your attention, mindset, attitude, focus, and ultimately your soul. And because these negative forces exist, you can expect great resistance to anything good, pure, wholesome, and positively productive.

Therefore, when I need to kick in the *Grateful Heart Principle* to bring everything back into prospective once again, it's undoubtedly the last thing I *feel* like doing. When I'm being bombarded with discouragement, blasted with issues, and the dark side is putting a magnifying glass over every problem that I'm facing, making them appear larger than life, the last thing I *feel* like doing is giving thanks!

That is why I say it's so simple, but not always so easy. For me personally, when I need help stepping back into a grateful position or mindset, I run to the most powerful source made available to everyone—the written Word of God, the Bible. The Bible is not just some old book that was merely written by various men of old. No, it is the infallible words of God. It has withstood every test, every trial, every scrutiny, and millions of people like me still live and breathe by its every word!

I cannot count the times when I have run to the Scriptures and found just the answer I needed, just the insight I longed for, just the piece of the puzzle that I was missing, and the very encouragement that I needed to carry on. I have found no other source—*and I have many*—that can even come close to this provision. No person, no philosophy, no amount of money or anything else can shift you into the *Grateful Heart Principle* when the storms of life are brewing.

It is simply the holy words of God that will make the difference every single time. It's your greatest source on earth and the very blueprints to build the greatest you! It will bring true contentment to your troubled heart. It will bring much needed rest to a weary soul—yet at the same time, neither is God's written Word an excuse to lay back or shrug off your part of the deal. You must press on with your newfound strength and your new attitude of gratitude, being thankful and being *still* within.

**The holy words of God
are the very blueprints
to build the *greatest* you!**

What people need more than anything in this fast-paced society in which we live is some inner stillness and rest. Yet at the same time, this inner rest allows us to continue to press forward and pursue the inner call of God on each of our lives to multiply, grow, expand, and prosper.

Again let me emphasize that being content is an attitude, not a license to quit! Being content means I'm thankful for where I am now, with a complete understanding that it is not where I'm going to stay. And even if I'm doing OK and all my needs are met, contentment doesn't for a second negate what God spoke over humanity from day one—the commission to press past being OK and to multiply.

I believe Adam and Eve understood this quite well. Even though they technically had everything they needed, they still knew they weren't placed in that Garden for a life of vacation. They understood that they were created in the image of Almighty God, and that in order to be a correct representation of Him, they too needed to create, design, and sow; they needed to multiply! So as they enjoyed the blessing of the Garden and as they appreciated everything that God had given them, they also began to follow the command of the Lord to expand and exceed in abundance.

I must be content—*yes*, that means having an attitude of gratitude, but I still must pursue God's divine principles and commands over my life to prosper! I must learn to be thankful for what I have right now, while having a full understanding that the best is yet to come!

Contentment is not settling for less! It's the recognition of blessings that I have been allowed to receive up to this point and an understanding that God has called me to press on into the land of more than enough!

The best is yet to come!

So many people today have misinterpreted the word *contentment* and now live in survival mode or, at best, maintain mode because they don't want to appear greedy or self-centered. However, this is terribly wrong and will leave individuals in a state of mind and a state of being which will never allow them to actually fulfill *all* of God's spoken words over them.

What's even more bothersome to me is this: I have met people who didn't really want much to do with Christianity because they had been presented a lifestyle of poverty and a path of trouble. How sad is that? How did we go from Genesis 1:28-29, where God is basically commanding us to prosper and be blessed abundantly, to millions of long-faced, "just hope I make it to Heaven" believers?

We will all face tough times. We will all go through tests and trials that we'd prefer not to have to endure. But far too many have settled for a life of tough times that enables them to live well below the expectations of their God-given destiny.

I do understand why people feel that prosperity is dangerous or ungodly. So many people have been stepped on, mistreated, and cast aside by someone else who cared more about their financial ambition than the value of a friendship or relationship. This in return has caused many well-meaning and good hearted individuals to look at the ambition of that person as the enemy, instead of making the individual accountable for their own selfish actions.

Many kindhearted individuals, who have been cast aside by greedy friends or relatives, have made the mistake of protecting the individual whom they loved by demonizing the things that the person pursued. Before long, new villains, named *money* or *prosperity*, arise from obscurity. In actuality, these don't have the ability within them to be villains; they are neutral. But it's easier to blame the money than to blame "my sweet, little, dear son who wouldn't hurt a fly."

After years of this, centuries of this, millenniums of this, we have all kinds of religions, mentalities, beliefs, and so forth that do not resemble anything close to the original *God Principles* released to humanity in the beginning and repurchased and established for us at Calvary. There are those who look down their long religious noses at those who have acquired great wealth, as if these individual have sinned in some way to gain what they have. Many even make the wealth itself a sin, saying things like, "How can you justify having all that money when people in the world are starving?"

This really takes us back once again to the reason that Jesus came to earth and died for all humanity. Most people have a basic understanding that Jesus did this so we could receive forgiveness for our sins, which is true. However, many fail to recognize that it is sin (AKA greed) that causes "my dear little son who wouldn't hurt a fly" to steal from me—not money or prosperity. Jesus didn't just die to pay for our sins and to become our sacrifice. No, there was more!

People had willingly and openly engaged in sinful activity, which ultimately stripped us of our full ability to prosper and multiply "without sorrow." This in return released the powers within sin, such as greed, jealousy, selfishness, and so much more, which after thousands of years, have created all kinds of fallacies and sects.

Many today are confused and are not sure what to believe or who to trust, and that is exactly the intended purpose of sin—to create a confused and misguided people who will ultimately shy away from the One who can give eternal life or who will connect to Him with a misguided and warped mindset that causes fear. At best, these individuals will miss all that they were destined.

Of course, there are the others who just don't care either way! They pursue their dreams, press into prosperity, grab hold of success with both hands, and live it up—only to wonder in the quietness of the night, *Why do I still feel empty?*

Jesus didn't just die to give us a path back home. He didn't just shed His blood that we might be forgiven and have everlasting life (which in and of itself is more than any of us deserve). No, my friends, there's more! Very few realize that when Jesus died He went to hell. You might be thinking, *Hey wait a minute, if He was perfect and sinless—and God for that matter— then how or why would He go to hell?* This is where it gets really interesting. He didn't go there because of sin or wrong doing or rejecting God's offer of salvation. He went there for a particular reason and for a distinct purpose. Jesus Christ descended into the depths of hell (according to the Scriptures) to recover something that people had willingly given away 4,000 years earlier (see Eph. 4:9).

As it was in the beginning, God still loved humankind with an unconditional love. Therefore, He still desired for humankind to "be fruitful and multiply and have dominion over the earth." So He went to hell to recover the keys (or the God-given ability) for people to do just that without sorrow. Humanity had handed the keys over to satan many, many years before, but Jesus went to get them back, and that's exactly what He did!

So Jesus didn't just come to save us; He also came to restore us to our fullest potential of representing Him! This is why Jesus boldly proclaimed that, *"…I've come that they may have life* [salvation]*, and that they may have it more abundantly* [restoration]*"* (John 10:10). Wow! What an amazing God! Not only has He made a way to eternal life, but He has also made a way to abundant blessings. Just that in itself should cause us to be content, thanking God each day for His amazing love for us.

Chapter 8

NEVER LOOK BACK

In this last chapter, I want to speak of the utmost importance of living a life of always *Believing Forward*. This may not sound too difficult to do right off the bat, but if you've been around awhile, if you've ever been through some serious storms, if you've ever been knocked down by the unforeseen circumstances of life, then you already know that the enemy of your soul works overtime in these situations. His favorite tactic is to come against you and make w*hat was* always look better than *what is* so you will stop believing for *what shall be.*

**It is important to live a life
of always *believing forward.***

There's an amazing story in the Bible about this very tactic and how quickly people will fall for it when trouble arises. This story is found in the fourth chapter of Numbers. It speaks about the time when the Israelites had just been led out of Egypt by Charlton Heston...I mean *Moses* (you know the story, right?).[1] Anyway, these people as a nation had just endured 400 years of slavery. They were not only physically in transition, but mentally and spiritually as well.

Everything started out miraculous. Not only had God delivered them through *signs and wonders*, such as the Red Sea parting, but they were excited because there was a new and fresh hope of a Promised Land where they would live, thrive, and be successful!

However, a journey of a thousand miles begins with one step, and then another, and then another. During the course of all those steps, and before you ever get to your place of destiny, you will inevitably face many challenges.

Even though everything started out so miraculous, it was only a matter of time before trouble hit and the head games began. After traveling in the desert for some time and after eating the same food every single day (which was supernaturally provided, by the way), the people began to complain and gripe and *look back to what was*. They said, "Remember the fish that we freely ate back in Egypt? Remember the cucumbers, garlics, melons, onions...now we have 'nothing' but this disgusting *manna*" (see Num. 11:5-6).

Do you see the mindset here? They started looking back and remembering this wonderful variety of food, but forgetting the slavery. When you get into a tough spot, when you go through a dry season, the enemy starts pulling you to look back through a distorted looking glass and to see the past in a slanted, partial way.

Now to be fair to these people, I can understand their dilemma. No one likes to *eat the same thing every day*, or to put it another way, *no one likes to feel stuck in a rut*. If you're not careful, just like the Israelites, you too will be tempted to look back in search for better days. But my friends, it's all a lie! Your miracle is always forward. Your breakthrough is always ahead, not behind! If the devil can get you looking back to what was, you will quickly forget about the Promised Land that lies ahead and the prosperity that shall be.

Manna was only the provision along the path to prosperity. Yet sometimes along the way, you will be tempted to focus on the provision instead of the promise. Indeed, you should be thankful for the provision, (that's what contentment is—an attitude of gratitude), but you should focus on the promise. Many times the deceiver will even try to hit you with condemnation, saying things to you like, "You should just be 'content' with what you have. Don't you know that you already have more than most?" However, he is not saying, "Be grateful"; he's implying, "Settle for what you have now and don't believe for anything more." That's what he wants people to think it means to be content. But the reality of contentment is having a grateful heart for what you have now, while continuing to believe that the best is yet to come!

I have found that many times in life, you will not be allowed to move forward until you first become thankful for what you have now. Here's the key: when you truly *believe forward* (which means you truly believe that the best is yet to come), then it's easy to be thankful for what you have right now. But when you don't believe forward, you become disgruntled and frustrated about what you have right now; and instead of being thankful, you complain! Thankfulness and contentment are in the hearts of those who truly believe forward. Murmuring and complaining are in the hearts of those who begin to look back.

God is all about progress. God is all about *Believing Forward*.

God is all about progress. God is all about *Believing Forward*. What most people fail to realize is this: when you begin to turn your heart back to what was and you start looking to the past and making statements like, "I wish I was back there…that's when things were really good," whether you realize it or not, you are making a declaration that, "The best has passed and the future holds nothing better than what I've already experienced."

These seemingly innocent statements ultimately question the very validity of God's Word, God's love for you, and God's plans for your life. And because you have been given the ability to create by your spoken words (according to the *Name It Principle* discussed in Chapter 1), you actually call into existence by your complaining a season of unproductive wandering. You literally throw yourself into an endless circling pattern.

This is why the Israelites wandered and circled in the same desert for 40 years! What's even more amazing is what it took to get them moving forward again. All the complainers, all those who had started to believe that what was behind was better than what still lay ahead, had to die off before everyone else could move forward.

Sometimes death is necessary for new life to begin! People don't like to talk about death too much, but many need some things to die off in their lives so they can move on to new things. Death to bad attitudes! Death to complaining and murmuring! Death to that old nature that tries to pull you down when you're desperately trying to go up! Death to the way things used to be! Death to those voices of the enemy that always try to cause confusion and strife!

Sometimes, you just have to draw your sword and put an end to the lies and manipulation of the *naysayers* so that you can once again start *Believing Forward*, because the best is yet to come! This is why the apostle Paul says that it can be a good thing to be a forgetful person every once in a while. He actually says this, *"...Forgetting those things which are behind...I press toward the goal..."* (Phil. 3:13-14).

What things, Paul? How about past mistakes, past regrets, past lifestyles, past wrong-thinking and negative mindsets? Forget all that stuff and embrace the possibilities that lie ahead. Set your mind on things above and refuse to look back. I can promise you that as soon as a hard time hits, as soon as a season of testing or molding comes along, if you're still spending time looking back and remembering *what was*, the devil is going to mess you up every time.

This is what he does. As soon as trouble hits, he starts warping your perspective and actual memory of how it really used to be. Pretty soon you have people thinking back to times that were bondage and slavery, but remembering them as fun and exciting.

Have you ever seen people do this? They start talking about something from 10 or 20 years ago like it was so great, and you're sitting there thinking, *Wait a minute, you were angry and frustrated living there. I seem to remember you not being very happy working at that place, but now you're telling everybody how great of a job that was.*

When people slip into this warped remembrance, they begin to forfeit the Promised Land, they begin to forfeit the blessings that are just ahead and the very best that God has to offer them, only to return to the chains of yesterday.

"Forgetting those things which are behind...." I always try to be very careful about how I remember the past, even the past blessings of the Lord. That might sound strange at first, but I've learned that if I'm not careful, the devil will even try to slip in and use the past blessings of the Lord as a discouragement. He'll say things like, "Remember when the Lord blessed you back then? You were so close to the Lord back then. I wonder where you went wrong? It doesn't seem like you're nearly as blessed today."

Sound familiar? The devil will even get religious on you and try to convince you that you were more spiritual *back then*. Your prayers were more effective *back then*. On and on he goes, but it's all a lie!

It's in those very challenging times when you must recognize his tactics, muster up every ounce of faith you have, jump to your feet, and loudly proclaim, *"The best is yet to come!"* It might sound crazy, but I promise you it will correct your path and keep you from getting sucked into another circling pattern. That's the enemy's goal, and that's why he tries so hard to get you looking back and thinking about what was.

Now I must clarify what I'm saying here. When I first started receiving this revelation, I thought, *What am I missing here?* I was sure that I was receiving this revelation from the Lord of *Believing Forward* and never looking back, but I felt as if there was a key missing because God had also said plainly many times, "Remember the things that I have done for you" (see Deut. 25:19; Ps. 78:8, 103:2; Isa. 46:9; John 16:4).

Over and over again I had read Scriptures where the Lord was saying, "Remember when I blessed you. Remember when I delivered you. Remember when I comforted you. Remember how I opened that door for you, brought you out, set you free." The list is nearly endless.

The key is this: remember with your eyes fixed straight ahead.

So what's the key? How can I remember the goodness of the Lord without putting myself at risk of getting pulled back into what was? I began to earnestly pray about this and meditate upon the Scriptures at hand. Suddenly the Lord spoke to me and said, "The key is this: remember with your eyes fixed straight ahead."

Suddenly I understood. *Remembering* and *looking back* are two very different things! To look back, you must turn your whole head around, which causes you to lose focus on that which is ahead. However, you can remember the goodness of the Lord with your eyes still fixed on the prize! You can remember His blessings while you still focus on the goal. You can remember His past mercy with your faith still intact and your vision still very much alive!

When you remember with your focus still ahead, you don't have to go back to *what was land* to pick up that memory, but rather, you force that past memory to come into the here and now—which builds your faith even more to believe for what you're still about to see! God is saying to His children, *"Remember what I've done, in order to believe for what I'm still going to do!"*

Forget those things which are behind, those things that are calling you, trying to get you to look back, but instead remember the goodness of the Lord that has been poured out upon you along the way. This will build your faith and cause you to reach forward. *Believe Forward* to the things that are still to come. Reaching forward is taking *Believing Forward* to the next level.

Now you're putting *feet* on your faith and *hands* on your vision. You're once again becoming a person of action who doesn't have time to go in another circle, but rather embraces each day with a breakthrough mentality that causes you to continually progress and prosper!

You're putting feet on your faith and hands on your vision.

It's vital that you understand that when you constantly believe forward and reach forward, you will feel resistance. Did you ever stick your hand out the window of your moving car as a child and feel the friction of the invisible air which caused your hand to shoot up and down wildly as you enjoyed the ride? *Believing Forward* can sometimes cause your faith to bounce around a little in the friction of the fast-moving atmosphere, just like your little hand did.

But no matter how fast the car was going, there was never enough resistance to rip your arm off. Even though you could angle you finger tips and cause your hand to shoot up or down, you were never in danger of losing your arm, because the connection to the rest of your body was greater than the resistance. When your *Believing Forward* begins to cause you to bump around a little in the fast-moving environment, just remember that your anchor is stronger than the resistance!

The reason you feel friction or resistance when you are *Believing Forward* is because what you see in the natural rarely lines up with what you're believing for. Therefore, you have to press toward the goal. You don't just walk right up to it, no problem. No, *you press* against the resistance, *you press* against the forces that would like to keep you down. That old limited mindset would like to limit you, *but you press.* Not everybody around you wants to move forward—which creates tremendous resistance, but you press to take hold of the very best that God has for your life, and the best is always forward!

God is a God of progress! Faith is a forward motion! Fear is faith working in reverse!

Both faith and fear ask you to believe in something that hasn't happened yet.

Faith and fear are more similar than you might think. Both have very similar attributes. Both faith and fear ask you to believe in something that hasn't happened yet! Faith asks you to believe that the *best* is yet to come. Fear asks you to believe that the *worst* is yet to come.

Fear says, "What if it doesn't work out?"

Faith replies, "What if it does? You're closer than you think."

Fear says, "It's so far away. You'll never get there."

Faith declares, "Your promotion is just around the corner."

Fear says, "You could get laid-off tomorrow."

Refuse to allow fear to pull you backward. Refuse to allow your head to be turned away from the possibilities of today and tomorrow. Remember the good, but focus on what lies ahead!

There's a very interesting story found in the Book of Genesis about a man named Lot. In this story, we read about Lot and his family (who were related to Abraham, the father of faith) living in the wicked cities named Sodom and Gomorrah. I suppose they had chosen to live there many years earlier because of convenience or future possibilities; the story does mention that the land there was very fertile.

However, these cities grew increasingly wicked and perverse, partaking in things that might even make some of our modern-day liberals blush with shame. So God sent two angels to rescue this family (which is a story in and of itself that God will always send rescue to good people living in rough places). The angels came to this family's house, told them they must flee, and after they gathered their things, proceeded to escort those who were willing out of the city. At the same time, these angels gave them strict orders to "not look back." The angels almost had to drag the family from the city. Yet in the process, the Lot's wife looked back and was instantly turned into a pillar of salt (see Gen. 19:1-29).

There's so much to learn from this story, but what I want to focus on here is this question: *What must have been going through this woman's mind before she looked back?* I'm not saying this in a condemning sort of way like, *what in the world was she thinking?* But rather in a quest to further understand: *I wonder what she was thinking?*

The first thing that comes to my mind is the fact that not all of her family wanted to leave. Two of her married daughters and her sons-in-law thought this was the stupidest thing that they ever heard! I'm sure the angels appeared in the form of ordinary men, and her older married children just weren't buying it. I imagine that her married daughters had children, so now we introduce grandchildren into the equation.

I have a feeling that they were all in her mind as these two strangers (angels) rushed them away. The indications of the story lead me to believe that they had done well over the years. They had built a life for themselves, they had planned a future in this place, so what must have been running through her mind that day?

If I had to take a guess, I would say that she was probably thinking, *I'm running toward nothing and running away from everything! Ahead is only the clothes on my back and a few measly belongings, behind is my home, my livelihood, everything I've worked hard to acquire. Ahead is the unknown, the unfamiliar; behind is the life I've come to know and love—this doesn't make any sense!*

Yet in the spiritual realm and through the eyes of faith, ahead were life, a future, and endless possibilities! Ahead was a reconnection with God and His ways and His plans for true prosperity that are not tainted with sin and sorrow. Behind was complete wickedness, endless circling, separation from God, and certain death. But fear had captured her mind, and just like faith, it demanded an action! Therefore, she "looked back" and was turned into a pillar of salt, or in other words, that which has no more value.

Fear will try to hold you in a place that has no more life in it for you! Fear will try to keep you holding on to things that once blessed you, but are now *what used to be* instead of *what can still be*. Fear will tempt you to look back, which will put you in direct opposition to God's words over your life!

This story in the very first book of the Bible, Genesis, had such powerful implications that Jesus Himself referred to it as He delivered a sermon one day to a large crowd. He simply said three words, *"Remember Lot's wife"* (Luke 17:32 KJV).

Jesus declared earlier in the Scriptures with complete clarity that those who put their hands to the plow and then "look back" are not fit for the Kingdom of God (see Luke 9:62 KJV). He was not saying that if you've ever looked back that you are not going to have a place in the Kingdom of God. If that was the case, we'd all be in trouble. No, He was saying that as long as you are looking back, you'll never be *fit*, meaning, *in position* or *in your proper place* to enter in.

It is impossible to plow a straight line looking back! You must look far ahead to a fixed landmark and keep your eyes focused on it. So many people are plowing lines that look like pretzels because they don't have their eyes fixed on an unmovable, unchanging force. Everyone wants to go to Heaven, but many have forgotten that the Bible teaches us that straight is the way and narrow is the gate that leads to eternal life (see Luke 3:4, 13:24; Matt. 7:14).

That means you must believe forward with your eyes focused on the only unchanging force, Christ Jesus, plowing a straight line that leads to better things, because the best is yet to come!

I believe that God, in His tremendous mercy toward all of us, is constantly sending angels and constantly acting on our behalf with the intention of keeping us focused and keeping us progressing throughout our lives.

I believe one of those God interventions happened to you when you picked up this book. Even now, God is leading you out of endless circles and debilitating mindsets. Let Him lead you out of difficult times and painful seasons. Open your mind to the joys of today and the endless possibilities of tomorrow. Take hold of these *God Principles* today and never look back! Start *Believing Forward* right now; it will change your life forever!

Activate God's Favor

Lord, transform my mind to think constructive and not destructive thoughts. Work with me and teach me how to create and establish a blessed life through my spoken words. Examine my heart and renew a right spirit within me that I may be able to walk in Your true calling over my life. Let Your Holy Spirit remind me to continue to speak life daily and prepare me to walk in my God-given fullest potential.

*Lord, I speak in faith, calling out to _____
(the job, your vision, your goal) that Your abundant
oils will flow and prosper the work of my hands. Doors
that were once closed will now be open! I declare
supernatural favor over my _____ (project,
business, finances) that I may bring You glory in all
that I do. Search me, Lord, that You may use and
multiply what I already have. Purify my heart and help
me to take full responsibility over my life and to stop
blaming others for where I am. Thank You, Lord, for
Your mercy that is new every day! I release and forgive
all those who have hurt me in the past. Allow Your
oil to flow freely over my life and all my endeavors.
Surround me with people who follow You and who are
successfully and divinely appointed to me.*

*Lord, bless me with a Joshua anointing, that I may
have a decided heart like him and that my vision will
align with Your will. Thank You for all the blessings
You have already released in my life. Help me to keep
an attitude of gratitude and to always be content, yet
to continually strive to multiply for Your Kingdom.
Beginning today, I will start Believing Forward and
stop looking to the past in comparison.*

*Thank You, Jesus, for preparing me for the abundance
that is to come!*

In Jesus' name, amen.

Prayer of Repentance that Leads to Salvation

The greatest gift that God can ever give you still awaits if you have never known or professed Jesus Christ as your Lord and Savior. To begin your journey to a personal relationship with God, pray this prayer with all sincerity from the fullness of your heart:

Dear Lord Jesus, today I make a decision to turn away from the old paths and surrender my life to You! Lord Jesus, please forgive me right now of all my sin and change me from the inside out. Come into my heart, be the Lord and Savior of my life! Let Your blood that was shed for me on the cross wash over my soul, that I may be clean.

In Jesus' name, amen.

Endnote

1. *The Ten Commandments*, VHS (1956). Moses played by actor, Charlton Heston (October 4, 1923–April 5, 2008).

REVIEW

It takes *real* preparation to truly be able to handle and enjoy blessings.

Chapter 1: All *God Principles* need more than just a revelation, they also require participation. For Adam, before he could receive God's greatest gift for him, he had to work at it for a while. It took Adam naming all creatures into existence to meet his Eve; the Creator taught the created how to create and how to establish something through the spoken word. Your words are so powerful that when you speak your words put Heaven in motion.

Chapter 2: If you cannot learn to take responsibility over your own situation, your own life, or the position you are in right now, then it will most likely never change. There are many things that happen that you did not choose, but you must take 100 percent responsibility over how you respond or react. *Taking Responsibility* is a decision to take charge from this moment forward, starting *right now*. Refuse to let your history control your destiny!

Chapter 3: Learn to borrow, instead of money, the *ability (or know-how)* to make money. Reposition yourself to meet people and obtain opportunities. Find someone who is successful in your arena so you can pull and borrow and gather from their wisdom and experiences. Visit the library and gather the *empty pots* to multiply in your life. Begin your *new* kind of borrowing today!

Chapter 4: *Forgiveness* is not a gift that you give someone else. Forgiveness is a gift that you give yourself. Forgiveness is a divine law and a God principle, and when practiced, it empowers, it enlightens, and it advances the individual or the cause every single time. When you close the door to your past, God's Spirit will begin to flow in your life, causing you to be more productive, more positive, and more effective in everything you do.

Chapter 5: Indecision limits God in His ability to perform miracles in your life. Learn to make a decision and stick with it! Many times adversity is proof that you are on the right path. One of the best ways to keep a *decided heart* is to make sure the vision is worth the hassle.

Chapter 6: *Actions* create opportunity! When you look at the promises and blessings in the Bible, you will always find a prerequisite. There is a direct connection between doing and being blessed.

Chapter 7: Prospering and truly being blessed has to do with attitude, demeanor, and mindset. *Gratitude* causes you to operate in the correct mindset. This in return, draws the right people toward you, as well as the right opportunities and connections.

Chapter 8: It is important to live a life of always *Believing Forward.* To look back, you must turn your whole head around, which causes you to lose focus on that which is ahead. God is saying, *"Remember what I've done in order to believe for what I am still going to do!"*

ABOUT KEVIN BOYD

Kevin Boyd is Senior Pastor of Truth Christian Ministries International in Las Vegas, Nevada. He and his wife, Gayla, have also developed and own different successful businesses in the Las Vegas area. Through Kevin's nearly 20 years of ministry and business woven together, God has created a unique platform for Kevin to speak into the lives of thousands of businessmen and women alike—sharing with them the transforming power of God. Kevin and Gayla have a tremendous desire to lead people into *life more abundantly* by teaching and living firsthand divine *God Principles*. They have three amazing sons: Austin, Eastin, and Destin.

IN THE RIGHT HANDS, THIS BOOK WILL CHANGE LIVES!

Most of the people who need this message will not be looking for this book. To change their lives, you need to put a copy of this book in their hands.

> *But others (seeds) fell into good ground, and brought forth fruit, some a hundred-fold, some sixty-fold, some thirty-fold* (Matthew 13:8).

Our ministry is constantly seeking methods to find the good ground, the people who need this anointed message to change their lives. Will you help us reach these people?

> *Remember this—a farmer who plants only a few seeds will get a small crop. But the one who plants generously will get a generous crop* (2 Corinthians 9:6).

EXTEND THIS MINISTRY BY SOWING
3 BOOKS, 5 BOOKS, 10 BOOKS, OR MORE TODAY,
AND BECOME A LIFE CHANGER!

Thank you,

Don Nori Sr., Founder
Destiny Image
Since 1982

DESTINY IMAGE PUBLISHERS, INC.

"Promoting Inspired Lives."

VISIT OUR NEW SITE HOME AT
WWW.DESTINYIMAGE.COM

FREE SUBSCRIPTION TO DI NEWSLETTER

Receive free unpublished articles by top DI authors, exclusive discounts, and free downloads from our best and newest books.

Visit www.destinyimage.com to subscribe.

Write to: Destiny Image
              P.O. Box 310
              Shippensburg, PA 17257-0310

Call: 1-800-722-6774

Email: orders@destinyimage.com

For a complete list of our titles or to place an order
online, visit www.destinyimage.com.

FIND US ON **FACEBOOK** OR FOLLOW US ON **TWITTER.**

www.facebook.com/destinyimage   facebook
www.twitter.com/destinyimage   twitter